FINDING A FRIEND IN THE MIRROR

FINDING A FRIEND IN THE MIRROR

SHANE R. BARKER

Deseret Book Company
Salt Lake City, Utah

©1988 Shane R. Barker
Printed in the United States of America

No part of this book may be reproduced in any
form or by any means without permission in writing
from the publisher, Deseret Book Company,
P.O. Box 30178, Salt Lake City, Utah 84130.
Deseret Book is a registered trademark of
Deseret Book Company.

First printing September 1988
Second printing June 1989

Library of Congress Cataloging-in-Publication Data

Barker, Shane R.
    Finding a friend in the mirror / Shane R. Barker.
      p.   cm.
    Includes index.
    Summary: Provides advice and examples suggesting how young people
can develop self-esteem and a positive attitude in social
situations, school, sports, or artistic endeavors.
    ISBN 0-87579-178-6 : $9.95 (est.)
    1. Self-respect—Juvenile literature. [1. Self-respect.
2. Assertiveness (Psychology)] I. Title.
BF697.5.S46B36 1988
158'.1—dc19

                                    88-21743
                                      CIP
                                      AC

For Cody, Shanna, and Sheremie

CONTENTS

1 *RUNNING THE COLORADO*

FINDING A FRIEND IN THE MIRROR!

For a terrifying split second, I thought the boat was going to flip.

Shooting up from the rapids, it caromed against a wall of water and pitched onto its side. It tipped crazily, but the next instant was smashing back down into the foam. Water boiled all around, crashing over the sides and drenching everyone inside.

Jamming the throttle to the stops, I turned the boat and sent it slewing around a boulder in the middle of the river. We shot through the surge and bounced over the shallows. Then suddenly we were into smooth water again. It had taken less than ten seconds to shoot the stretch of white water, though it seemed more like ten minutes.

As I steered the boat over to shore to check for damage, a fourteen-year-old boy named Jeff jumped up onto the side of the boat.

"Wow!" he shouted. "That was great!"

"Sure was!" I agreed. "I'd say that was our best run yet."

Jeff's face was flushed with excitement. "How long till the next rapids?"

"Right around the corner," I said. "Right around the corner."

I had guided white water trips through the Grand Canyon before, but I couldn't remember having a passenger who was as enthusiastic as Jeff. He had a map of the Colorado River with all of the major rapids marked on it, and he spent time every day poring over it.

One time, as we were nearing one of the less dangerous stretches, I called to him. "Like to drive the boat through this one?"

Jeff's eyes lit up like Temple Square at Christmastime. "Really? Can I?"

"Sure! Why not?"

Jeff hopped into the back of the boat and listened as I showed him what to do.

"Just keep the boat in the middle of the river," I said. "And follow the current."

I showed him how to steer the boat, and then let him give it a try. He immediately opened the throttle and sent the boat slicing through the water.

"Hold on!" I said. "We'll pick up all the speed we need in a minute! For now, just let the river carry us along."

Jeff and I became great friends on that trip. He often sat in the back of the boat and talked with me as I drove. And we often spent time together at night. We talked about sports, mountains, rivers, and anything else that seemed interesting.

One night he walked over to me while I was preparing dinner, and we began talking about school.

"What grade are you going to be in this year?" I asked him. "Eighth?"

He shook his head. "Nope. I'm a big ninth grader this year."

"Ninth grade, huh? I remember being in ninth grade—best three years of my life."

Jeff laughed. "Did you like school?"

"Yeah, I did. I had a lot of friends, and I had pretty good teachers, too." I began warming up a dutch oven over a butane stove. "What about you?"

"Not really. I'm not very smart."

"Oh, yeah? Neither was I. But I got on the honor roll a couple of times."

Jeff looked interested. "How?"

"I just worked hard. Most of my friends were good students, and they all got good grades. I wanted to be like them, so I tried to get good grades, too."

After discussing school, we talked about Scouting. Jeff had earned his Star, but he didn't seem interested in pursuing his Eagle.

"Aw, big mistake," I said. "Earning your Eagle is a big deal. I'd go for it if I were you."

After a week, halfway down the Grand Canyon, Jeff's tour came to an end. The helicopter that brought in a new group of people took him and the rest of our passengers out of the canyon. Jeff's mother took me aside while they waited for their turn to leave.

"I want to thank you for all you've done for Jeff," she told me.

"Aw, he's a great kid," I said. "He's fun to have along."

"No, I mean about getting him excited about school."

I was confused. "What do you mean?"

"Jeff has never been a very good student," she

told me. "He's just never liked school. But after your talk he suddenly wants to be on the honor roll."

"I had no idea."

"You've got him excited about Scouting, too," she said. "He told me that he wants to get his Eagle."

I wasn't sure what to say. I liked Jeff a lot. And I considered him a good friend. But I had no idea that I was making such a powerful impression on him.

On the other hand, I've found that life is usually like that. We each have a tremendous influence on the people around us. But we often never even know about it.

Now, how about you? Have you ever had an influence on anyone?

I'll bet you have—even if you don't know it. Because *you* are a terrific person! You have great strengths and talents. And you *do* have an incredible influence on the people around you. And just because you don't see it happening, don't think that it's not true.

I have a friend who's the senior patrol leader of his Boy Scout troop. Ryan is a good leader, but he used to wonder if he was doing any good. The boys in the troop were all friends of his, but they were typical boys. They were rowdy in troop meetings, and even during important lessons they never seemed to pay any attention.

"It was really discouraging," Ryan told me. "I tried to make things as fun as I could, but nobody cared. Everything I taught them went in one ear and out the other."

What Ryan didn't know was that many of the boys

in the troop *were* listening. One of them was a Scout named Travis.

Travis was tending his brother and sister one day when his little brother fell through a glass window. The boy's left arm was cut deeply at the wrist, and within seconds the floor was covered with blood.

Not wasting any time, Travis put pressure on the boy's wrist, holding his bare hands against the wound. He yelled for his sister. "Quick! Get me a towel! Then call an ambulance!"

Taking the towel from his sister, Travis slapped it onto the wound and clamped it down as hard as he could. He kept the wound from bleeding until the paramedics arrived and took over.

Later on, doctors praised Travis for his quick thinking. They told him that he had done everything exactly right and that he had saved his brother's life.

"I just knew what to do," Travis said. "I learned it in Scouts!"

Ryan had taught the lesson the night Travis learned first aid. He didn't know that anyone was listening, but when a boy's life was in danger, Travis knew exactly what to do.

Ryan's lesson had saved a life.

Whether you know it or not, you make a difference in this world. A big one! As a young person, you come into contact with many people every day. And you can't associate with others without having some effect on them. Besides that, you have successes every day, many of which you may never know about.

So believe that you are a terrific person! Believe that you matter. Believe that you have the ability to blaze into life with the fury of a whirlwind and bless the lives of others.

I know a young woman named Jennifer who was a counselor at girls' camp. It was her first time as a leader, and she knew she was making mistakes. Even so, she soon made friends with a twelve-year-old camper named Holly.

Holly was the most bubbly, energetic young woman Jennifer had ever met. And having Holly around made Jennifer's own experience at camp much more fun.

At the end of the week, though, Holly had a surprise. Taking Jennifer aside she said, "Thanks so much for everything you've done for me."

Jennifer gave her friend a hug. "No, thank *you!* You've made the whole week for me."

Holly just smiled. And then she confided, "This is the first time I've ever been away from home. The first two days I was so homesick I begged Sister Anderson to let me go home. But after I made friends with you, I was okay."

Jennifer didn't know that. She thought *she* was the one being blessed by their friendship!

A young neighbor of mine named Terri was once being interviewed by her bishop. As they talked, the bishop told Terri how proud he was of her.

"You're a great example for the young women in the ward," he said. "Many of them watch everything you do."

At first, Terri thought he was just giving her the usual bishop's pep talk. But as he talked, she began to realize that he meant what he was saying.

"My own daughter talks about you all the time,"

he told her. "Do you remember the last time you cut your hair?"

Terri nodded.

"Well, Sarah loved it so much she went right out and had hers cut the same way. She wanted to look just like you!"

Remember that people are watching you, too. People see what you wear to school, and they listen to the jokes you tell. They notice the way you act, and they watch the way you treat people. And many times they'll do things just because they've seen you do them. You may never know it, but it's true.

I once spent a summer working at a Boy Scout camp with a young man named Brad. He was one of the finest young men I've ever known, and he was one of my best friends. We shared a tent that summer, and we spent time every night talking, telling stories, and making plans. Besides that, we went hiking together, fishing together, and Scouting together.

Brad was such an influence on me, in fact, that I followed his example in many ways. Because of him I began reading scriptures each night before bed. And when I said my prayers at night, I often prayed for help in living my life as well as Brad lived his life. I wanted to live and act so that people would think as highly of me as I thought of Brad.

One day I noticed that Brad was acting a little sad. When I asked what was wrong, he just shook his head.

"Sometimes I just don't feel like I'm doing any good," he said. "Sometimes I just don't feel like I'm getting anywhere."

I couldn't believe it. Brad was one of the best

7

friends I'd ever had. And I had more respect and admiration for him than for almost anyone else I knew. He *was* doing good . . . even though he didn't know it!

Like Brad, we don't always see all of the good that we do. We don't see all the impressions that we make, and we don't see all our successes. And because of that we sometimes get discouraged.

But don't let that happen to you. Remember that *you* are a wonderful person. You have a great effect on people. You are loaded with talents and abilities. You achieve successes every day.

Not only that, but people like you. People look up to you. People admire you. You may not know it, but *you* are somebody's best friend. You are somebody's favorite person.

And if you can be those things for someone else, you can certainly be them for yourself!

The next time you see yourself in a mirror, try this: look yourself straight in the eye and say out loud, "I like you!" Then say it again. And again. Say it louder now . . . and mean it.

You are a terrific person. And you owe it to yourself to be your own best friend.

How to Get Started!

- Go find a mirror . . . right now! Look yourself straight in the eye and say, "I make a difference!" Now say it again. Then say, "I am important!" See if you don't start to feel a surge of confidence.

- When you get up in the morning, go right to the mirror and look yourself straight in the eye again. Then say, "I like you!" Say it again, and again. And *mean it!*

- Now take a 3 x 5 card and write, "I like you!" on it. (Or, if you want to be a little different, write, "I'm No. 1!") Tape this card to your mirror and read it every day. Put another one in your locker at school, or anywhere else that you'll see it often. Read it whenever you feel like you need a boost.

- Remember always that *you* are important. Remember that you make a difference in this world. You may never see all the good you do, but remember that it's there!

- Think of someone who likes *you* more than he or she likes anyone else. Remember that *you* are his or her very favorite person. And remember if you can be a favorite person for someone else, you can be that for yourself!

2 *TRIPPING WITH THE BASKETBALL*

LOOKING FOR THE BEST IN YOURSELF

*D*avid Lesher was grinning as he stepped to the side of the serving lane and lobbed the racquetball down the court. BAM! The ball slammed into the wall and shot straight back, hitting the floor just behind the serving line only inches from the wall.

Lunging out with my racquet, I tried to backhand the ball but succeeded only in smashing my racquet against the wall.

David laughed. "Okay, what does that make the score? Fifteen — three?"

"Fourteen — three, and I don't want to hear about it," I growled.

David laughed again as he returned to the serving lane and set up for his next serve. I hated his wallpaper shots. I had such a terrible backhand that I could never hit them, and I had enough trouble playing against David as it was.

But David knew that, and that's why he served them so often. He had a few other tricks he enjoyed tormenting me with, too.

"Watch this," he said one time as he set up in the lane. He was standing in right center court, and he smacked the ball diagonally across the floor.

BA-BAM!

The ball ricocheted off the front wall and against the side wall, shooting back across the court so that it hit the opposite side wall deep in the backcourt about waist high. The ball had so much down spin that it dropped right into the back corner.

I was so surprised that I just stood in the middle of the court without even making a try for it.

David laughed. "Ace," he said.

Sometimes I wondered why I liked playing with David. I had only beaten him once in my life (when he played the whole game left-handed). And he was so much better than me that he usually made me feel like a clod.

But racquetball wasn't the only thing that David could beat me at. He could outshoot me in basketball, outrun me in track, and outhit me in baseball. Besides that, he was faster than I was, smarter than I was, and better looking than I was. He used to console me by saying, "Yeah, but everybody's better looking than you are!"

David had so many talents, in fact, that I often envied him. I wanted to play racquetball the way he did. I wanted to run as fast as he could and shoot baskets as well as he could.

David was one of my best friends in the world. But being around him was often depressing. He was so good at so many things that he made me feel like a klutz.

And it was a long time before I learned that I didn't need to compare myself with him.

I mean, sure, he could play racquetball. But I could scuba dive. And sure, he could run a marathon. But

I could fly an airplane. Sure, he was better looking than I was. But like he said — everybody was better looking than I was!

My problem was that I spent too much time comparing myself with David, when we really weren't all that much alike. Both of us had different skills and talents. And it wasn't fair to compare my abilities against his. He had his strengths, and I had mine.

When you see the skills and talents of others, it's easy to want to measure yourself against them. But you can't do that, especially when your own skills and talents are different from those of the people around you. The trick is learning to focus on the good that's in *you*.

Now I know that looking for the best in yourself isn't always an easy thing to do. After all, life has a way of pointing out our faults and weaknesses while hiding our strengths and talents. We all know what things are wrong with us, and sometimes we have a hard time figuring out what's right with us.

So let's look at a couple of keys for unlocking the talent and potential that's within you.

The first key is to learn to appreciate your own worth.

Sure, you might have a skinny face. But maybe you've got a great smile. And maybe you can't sing. But maybe you have an untapped ability for playing the piano.

The fact that you aren't a starting quarterback is no reflection on your qualities as a person. So learn to think of things you are, rather than of things you are not.

I have a neighbor named Tony who plays on his

high school basketball team. Right in the middle of a close, heated game one time, he made a steal in the enemy backcourt.

As quick as a cat, Tony turned and bolted down the floor. He should have had an easy layup. But halfway down the court—with no one even near him—he tripped and fell flat on his face. The ball went spinning out of bounds, and the crowd erupted in laughter.

Now how would you have felt right then? Pretty dumb? I would have!

But Tony picked himself off the floor laughing. He shook his head, grinned sheepishly, and bowed to the crowd before returning to the game.

"You bet I felt dumb," he told me later. "But, hey— I was playing a good game. I wasn't going to let one mistake bother me."

What a great attitude! Tony recognized his value to the team. He knew that the same people who saw him trip also saw him score seventeen points. He appreciated his own worth enough to know that a minor mistake wasn't going to hurt anything.

You need to be like that. If you happen to trip up once in a while, don't fret over it. Remember the points you've scored! Learn to focus on your good points, not your bad ones.

The second key is to think only good thoughts about yourself.

Nothing is more damaging to your self-esteem than doubts and negative thoughts. So learn to refuse them just as you would refuse a drink or a cigarette. In a very real sense, negative thoughts are every bit as damaging as alcohol or tobacco.

13

I remember once having a bad day at work. I was supposed to do some writing that evening, but my mind was so full of sour images that I couldn't work. I let a few negative thoughts cloud and pollute my mind so that I wasted an entire night.

Controlling your thoughts takes an enormous amount of self-discipline. But it's possible. And the best way to do it is by filling your mind so full of good, positive images that there's no room for the negative ones.

I know a young woman named Loralee who was having a hard time at school. Several girls teased her constantly. They talked about her when she was close enough to hear, and they laughed when she passed them in the hall. It hurt her feelings terribly. She steamed over it during the day, and she brooded about it at night.

But then one day she realized that she had friends. Lots of them! So whenever the thought of her enemies began to bother her, she simply began thinking about her friends.

One night, when she just couldn't seem to get her enemies off her mind, she began thinking about a special friend named Shelley. Shelley had been especially good to her. And Loralee began thinking of nice things she could do in return. It wasn't long before her enemies had all been forgotten.

Somewhere in your life you're certain to have some good, positive, uplifting memories, too. Use them! Whenever you start to feel less than you really are, remember successes you've had. Think about fun people you've met and great times you've had. Refuse to dwell on negative thoughts and experiences.

The third key is always to be you at your best.

Many times in your life you will have to make decisions. Sometimes you'll make the wrong ones, and later on you'll feel bad about them. But what's worse than that is making wrong decisions when you *know* they're the wrong decisions.

Whenever you feel tempted to make a wrong decision, picture your best self. Picture yourself as you would like to be, and how you would like others to see you. And try to picture that terrific person making the wrong choice. It's hard to do, isn't it?

When I was in high school, my grandfather took a picture of me. Now I usually don't turn out very well in pictures, but this one made me look great. It made me look the way I wanted to look. I used to keep it in a drawer, and sometimes I'd look at it before going to school. It was a picture of me at my best, and seeing it made me feel at my best. I'd think of it during the day and let it bring out the best in me.

Do the same thing yourself. Keep a mental picture of your best self handy. Use it to motivate yourself during hard times. Use it to sustain yourself during sad times. Use it to bring your best self out.

The final key is to give yourself a pat on the back once in a while.

I know a young woman named Amy who one night played a saxophone solo as part of the school Christmas concert. And she was wonderful! She played with so much expression and energy that everyone in the audience knew she was having fun. They knew she was enjoying herself. And that enhanced her performance.

Later, people crowded around her to offer compliments.

"Amy, that was great!"

"You were terrific!"

"Your solo was *so* good!"

Amy was a humble, down-to-earth young woman. But this night she smiled broadly and said, "It *was* good, wasn't it?"

Amy wasn't bragging that night. It wasn't in her nature to brag. But she *had* done a good job, and she was giving herself a pat on the back for it.

Don't be afraid to do the same yourself!

When you have successes, reward yourself for them. Don't file them away where they're going to be forgotten, but relive them from time to time. Let the excitement of past successes build your self-esteem. Let them inspire you to do similar things again.

Remember that you *are* special. Remember that you are loaded with potential and personality. Sometimes it's easy to forget that. And sometimes it's hard to find those things that are right with you.

But don't give up trying! Learn to appreciate your value to your friends and family. Think only positive things about yourself. Always be you at your best. Give yourself a pat on the back once in a while.

Most of all, tell yourself that you're okay! And do it often. As you do, you'll come to discover that there is a wealth of good within you. You'll find that you really do have a friend in the mirror.

How to Get Started!

- Learn to appreciate your worth! When you wake up in the morning, tell yourself, "I'm okay." And if you ever trip up, tell yourself, "That's okay." Learn to remember the points you've scored, not the points you've missed.

- Refuse to think negative thoughts. The next time you begin feeling bad about yourself (or the next time you doubt your ability to do something) drive those thoughts out of your mind! Think of positive things! Fill your mind so full of good, positive thoughts that there's no room for negative ones!

- Always be you at your best! Never do anything that you know you'll be ashamed of later. Keep in your mind a picture of your best self, and think of it every time you feel tempted to do something you know you shouldn't.

- Give yourself a pat on the back once in a while! Tell yourself that you're okay! And do it often! Reward yourself for all of the great things you do!

3 *STUTTERING ON THE TELEPHONE*

LOOKING PAST YOUR HANGUPS

*C*hris Hansen looked up as a drop of rain splattered over his plateful of French toast. He wrinkled his face like he'd taken a whiff of sour milk.

"Man," he said. "This rain is starting to ruin my life!"

I looked up as a crack of thunder rolled in from the distance and nodded. This was our third day at Boy Scout Camp, and for the third day in a row the rain was going to ruin nearly every merit badge class we had scheduled. Lightning would keep us from swimming or going out on the lake. And the muddy runoff was certain to spoil the fishing.

It looked like we were doomed to spend the day in our tents when my friend Cannon suddenly had an idea.

"Let's go to the rifle range and see if they'll let us shoot. It's too wet for targets, but maybe they'll let us have an egg shoot!"

"An egg shoot?"

"Sure—everybody sets up an egg and shoots at it." His eyes twinkled mischievously. "And everybody who misses has to eat it . . . raw."

The troop was instantly enthusiastic. And so was

the rifle range director. (It turned out that he was as bored as anyone.) We spent more than an hour blazing away at eggs and laughing as those who missed swallowed them raw.

After our egg shoot we put on our swimming suits and spent the next little while playing frisbee football out on the meadow. By the time we were finished we were as wet as if we had just been swimming, and we were covered with mud. But our scoutmaster had thought ahead and had a blazing fire and a steaming pot of hot chocolate ready for us. That afternoon we pulled on our ponchos and played steal the flag in the forest.

The rain didn't let up the entire time we were at camp. And we missed out on many activities we had been looking forward to. But in many ways the rain made our trip more adventuresome. We got to do and try things we never would have thought of if the weather had been clear. We learned that there *were* fun things to do when it rained. While other troops sat in their tents and sulked, we went out and created our own adventures.

Many of us often face personal experiences just like that. After all, we all have troubles, and we all have problems. And we all have hangups that get in the way of our progress.

But the real problem is that sometimes we get so caught up in what's wrong in our lives that we never stop to look for what's right. We worry so much about our faults that we never get to know our strengths. We fret so much over the things we can't do that we never get good at the things we can do.

Learn now to look beyond your hangups! Learn

to look beyond your weaknesses so that you can focus on your strengths.

When I was in college I worked part-time as a sportswriter, and I often shared information with a man named Rick at a rival university. Rick always knew what was going on around the country, and he could always fill me in on team rankings, stats, and other information I needed for my stories.

The only problem was that when I get nervous, I tend to stutter a little bit. And Rick always made me nervous. He had a precise, rapid-fire way of speaking that made him seem like he was in an incredible hurry, and I usually ended up talking like I had a mouthful of marbles.

Sometimes I would be working in my office when the phone would ring and Rick would be on the other end. I would answer casually.

"Hello, Sports Information."

"Hello,Shane,thisisRickMarshall. Howyadoin'? ListenIneedsomeinformation. Ineedtoknowwho wastheleadingscoreronyour women's basketball team againstWashingtonlastweek!"

"Sh . . . Sh . . . Sheery . . . Sherry Daniels," I would finally blurt out.

No matter when Rick called, he always caught me by surprise. And I always ended up saying something dumb to him. One time I became so flustered talking with him that I gave him the wrong line scores. I had to call him back later to correct the mistake.

Phoning him was just as bad. I took a great deal of time to prepare for the call, forming my questions and having everything I needed right at hand where I could get at it easily.

But even though I was ready, I often spent ten minutes or more just gathering up enough courage to make the call. I didn't want him to think I was a nerd. And I dreaded talking with him.

One day, though, I phoned while he was out of the office. I ended up having a nice conversation with his secretary, and she told me something I never would have dreamed of.

"Rick really likes the way you write," she told me.

"Really?"

"Oh, yes. He keeps every story you send him. Sometimes he reads them when he's stuck for a good lead or a new idea."

I was flattered and humbled at the same time. For the first time I realized that Rick didn't care about my imperfect speech. He admired my skills as a writer.

And that's all that really mattered.

It occurred to me later that I wasted a good deal of time worrying about the way I talked, when I was the only one who cared! I spent more time worrying about my hangups than I spent improving my talents. I realized that everyone else was looking past my hangups . . . so why shouldn't I?

I have a friend named Jennifer who had a similar experience. A junior in high school, Jennifer had a beautiful soprano voice. She could fill a song with power and feeling one moment, then sing as softly as a whisper the next.

But Jennifer was also overweight. And she was so sensitive about her appearance that she wouldn't consider auditioning for solos at school concerts. She was so self-conscious that the thought of being seen alone on stage terrified her.

Her parents tried everything they could think of to convince her to audition, but it wasn't until the school Christmas concert that she finally agreed. She won the part easily, and the night of the concert she sang the solo part of "Silent Night." I was there that night, and I cried as she sang.

She was that good.

Jennifer knew that she had talents. But she let her fear keep her from improving them. It was a long time before she learned to look beyond her hangups so that she could develop her talents to their fullest.

Like Jennifer, you've got a few hangups, too. Maybe you've got a whole lot of them. But the important thing to remember is that everyone has problems. Everyone! Some people may have the same problems you have. Others may have an entirely different bunch. But whatever the case, you can't let your hangups rule your life. You've got to learn to work around them.

When I was in high school I often played basketball with a boy named Mike. He was quick on his feet, good with his hands, and sure on the floor. He could dribble better than anyone on the high school team, and he never seemed to tire. He could play all over the court, running the fast break and then dashing back down the floor to set up on defense without even working up a sweat. He was a terror to play against.

Mike's only problem, in fact, was that he was just five foot three.

Mike never let his lack of height affect him. After all, there was nothing he could do about it. All the stretching exercises in the world wouldn't help. And the most potent vitamins known wouldn't make him grow.

So Mike concentrated on the skills he *did* have. He knew he was quick, and he knew he had good hands. He knew he had a good eye for the basket. So he developed these skills. He looked beyond his hangups to develop his strengths.

To reach your fullest potential, you must do the same.

It's hard finding the good in yourself when you're focused on your hangups. But if you really want to discover the best in yourself, you've got to look past your weak points and zero in on your strong ones.

I once saw a young woman play a trumpet solo during a junior high school band concert. She was good, too. She played with a sharp, clear tone and a range that was rare for a musician her age.

But the most unusual thing about her was that she had only one arm.

Now I play the trumpet, too. And I know how difficult it is to play with only one hand. It's fortunate that this young woman was able to look beyond her personal difficulty to develop the musical skills her Heavenly Father had given her.

If you have problems that can't be worked out, then accept them. Learn to live with them. Find ways to work around them. Most important, don't worry about them. Concentrate instead on the skills and attributes you *do* have.

When I was in high school I had a friend who was deaf. Allison never heard a word her teachers said, but she was a straight A student. Though her ears didn't function, she refused to let that stop her. She had other senses, and she used them to their fullest.

Remember that no one is perfect. *Everyone* has problems. And if that's all you're looking for in yourself, that's what you're sure to find.

But there's no point in that. Instead, look for the good. Look carefully! Your face may be a trifle plump, but maybe you've got pretty eyes. You may be short for your age, but maybe you're the fastest runner in the school. Be brave enough to find out!

While you're busy looking beyond your hangups, forget about past mistakes you've made, too. There's nothing like a few slipups from the past haunting you to make you feel lousy. But what's past is past. Learn to remember that and to get on with your life.

On a cross-country ski trip once, I became friends with a twelve-year-old boy named Chuck. He was polite, funny, interesting, and enthusiastic. We spent many hours together, and I came to like him very much.

Near the end of the trip, one of Chuck's leaders came to thank me for the time I was spending with my new friend.

"Chuck's been through some tough times," he told me. "And he has a history of shoplifting."

That didn't bother me. I liked Chuck. And mistakes he had made in the past didn't change the way I felt about him.

Remember that we learn through experience. And it's impossible to progress without making a few mistakes along the way. If you've slipped up at times, don't let those mistakes haunt you. Forget them! Repent, if you need to, but don't let past slipups stand in the way of your progress now.

Several years ago I was attending a party with some friends when I did some things that were pretty silly. I know that everyone there thought for sure that I was a nerd.

I used to think back on that night and kick myself for being so stupid. For a long time, the thought of it made me cringe. But there was no use worrying about it. I learned my lesson, and I don't let it bother me anymore.

As you look for the good in yourself, learn to look beyond your hangups. Learn to focus on the things you *can* do. Forget about mistakes you've made and look forward with confidence.

As you do, you'll find that your life is full of good. Best of all, you'll find that you *can* have fun when it rains!

How to Get Started!

- Think of three things you've done that you're proud of. Think back several years if you need to, but come up with three great things that you've accomplished. Now write them down. And the next time you begin worrying about your hangups, read your list. Remember that if you've done great things before, you can certainly do them again.

- Now think of three things that are right about you. Think hard! Maybe you're good in math. Maybe you're a good listener. Or maybe you just try hard. See? If you think hard enough, you're bound to come up with three things. Now write them down. Think about them whenever you begin to have doubts about yourself.

- Promise never to kick yourself again for mistakes you've made. Remember that what's past is past. Repent, if you need to, and resolve to do better the next time. Then learn to look forward in life, not backward.

- Most important, refuse to let doubts and negative thoughts pollute your mind. Fill your mind with your positive qualities.

4 *JOINING THE POLAR BEAR CLUB*

TURNING WEAKNESSES INTO STRENGTHS

*T*yler Dixon took a last lungful of the cool mountain air and then leaped from the dock into the lake. He disappeared as the water closed over his head but was up the next second gasping for breath.

"Ah . . . ah . . . ah . . ." he gasped. "It's . . . c . . . c . . . cold!"

Robert Walker laughed. "Okay, Tyler. The hard part's over. Now let's see if you can swim."

Shaking his hair free of water, Tyler sucked in another deep breath, then began swimming for a point fifty feet away. He got there with no problem, and he made the return trip on his back to complete his swim easily. He was met by a chorus of cheers.

"All right, Tyler!"

"Way to go, Tyler!"

"Good job out there!"

The fourteen-year-old boy pulled himself from the water and wrapped himself with a beach towel.

"Wow," he said with a grin. "That was cold!"

Robert, the aquatics director of the high adventure base, handed the boy a steaming cup of hot chocolate and hung a leather cord around his neck. Hanging from the cord was a plastic bear claw wrapped in a bit of white fur.

"There," Robert said. "I pronounce you an official member of the Three Creeks Polar Bear Club."

I was standing on the dock watching the ceremony, and I couldn't help but smile as Robert turned and sent the next boy into the lake. Before allowing anyone to participate in his water activities, Robert was required to test each camper's swimming ability. The test was a simple one-hundred-foot course through smooth water. But because this was a high mountain lake, the water was very cold. Campers didn't mind boating on it. They didn't mind jumping from the camp's lava cliffs into it. And they didn't mind playing in it. But when it came to taking the required swim test, no one wanted to participate.

Not, that is, until Robert came along.

Robert knew from the start that he would have trouble administering his test. So he took the idea of a test and changed it into a challenge. He formed a Polar Bear Club for everyone brave enough to swim one hundred feet in the cold mountain lake.

And the kids loved it. They were as excited at becoming Polar Bears as they were at diving off cliffs. Robert had taken one of his biggest headaches and turned it into one of his most popular activities.

Many of us often face dilemmas similar to Robert's. Sometimes we're faced with tasks that seem impossible. And many times we have more personal challenges, such as big ears or skinny legs. But just as Robert did, we can take our greatest challenges and turn them into our greatest strengths.

I know a barber, for instance, who has no hair.

Think about that for a minute. How would you like having your hair cut by a bald barber? That's almost like having a ski instructor with a broken leg. It doesn't do a lot for your confidence, does it?

Well, Mr. Jenkins could have solved his problem in a couple of ways. He could have spent a lot of time worrying about how his baldness would affect his ability to cut hair. He could have bought a wig to cover his head.

But he had a novel approach. He proudly took his bare head to work every day and cut people's hair to the best of his ability. And whenever anyone asked about his baldness, he'd just point to his head and say, "This is what happened the last time I let someone besides me cut my hair!"

That's good thinking!

It's best not to dwell on your faults and shortcomings. After all, you're sure to have just as many strengths and talents, and you might as well be concentrating on them.

But if you do have a fault or two that you just can't keep off your mind, try turning them into assets.

When I was in high school I had a friend named Gary who owned the oldest, noisiest, ugliest car I have ever seen. It was painted a flat shade of purple, and the finish was so dull you couldn't see the sun reflecting from it on even the brightest of summer days.

But that wasn't all. The car was fitted with huge, bulging headlights that poked out like the eyes of a big bug. The tires stuck out from the sides, and the front end was jacked up higher than the rear. When it was going down the road, the car looked like an airplane going for takeoff.

We used to tease Gary about his car, but it was the only one he could afford to own. It was the one he had to drive to school. It was the one he had to drive to work. And, yes, it was the one he had to drive on dates.

Now when I was in high school, we worried about the cars we drove. They were a major part of our lives. And I don't know how you would feel about going on dates in a car like that, but Gary approached the problem in an unusual way.

He made the car *fun!*

Whenever a group of us went anywhere, Gary volunteered to drive. So we often showed up at ball games, dances, and parties in his horrible purple car. When we had our homecoming parade, he decorated it and used it as a float. And at the football game later that day, Gary seated the homecoming royalty on the hood and drove them around the football field.

He made his car famous.

Even at school, Gary refused to park near the back of the school lot. Instead, he'd park right on the front row where everybody could see. He made it clear that he *liked* his car!

Gary's plan worked so well that when the junior prom came and we were all dressed in tuxedos, we decided to go in Gary's car, even though we could have borrowed nicer, newer cars. Riding in Gary's car had become a status symbol. And even our dates were delighted to attend the formal dance in the battered old bomb.

Gary could have been ashamed of his car. But he

turned a weakness into a strength. He looked for a positive approach to the problem. He made his car's ugliness work *for* him.

There was nothing magical about Gary's approach. It was just a matter of attitude. Rather than be ashamed of his car, Gary was proud of it. And he magnified his pride to such lengths that his enthusiasm spread.

I have a friend named Kamron who plays football. One morning when we were driving to school, I noticed that he was a little quieter than usual.

I asked him if anything was wrong.

"I've just got a headache," he said.

"Anything I can do to help?"

Kamron shook his head, then changed his mind. "Well, why don't you stop and let me out. I'll just run it off."

It worked, too. Kamron showed up at school a short time later feeling great. Rather than let a headache ruin his day, he had gone out and done something positive about it.

That's the same thing you must do. Don't let your problems, shortcomings, and hangups rule your life. Instead, rule them! Do something positive about them. Let them work for you.

I happen to have a difficult time matching clothes. People who don't worry about hurting my feelings often tell me that I have no taste.

This might not sound like a very big deal to you, but dressing nicely is important to me. One night, as I was preparing to attend a ward fireside, my sister looked at what I was wearing and began to laugh.

"Are you really going to wear that?" she asked. "Or are you trying to be funny?"

I was crushed. I had given a lot of thought to what I was wearing that night, and it hurt to learn that I was so wrong. My sister explained that striped ties don't match plaid shirts, and that blues and greys don't look all that good together, and I shuddered to think how I must have looked.

Buying clothes is just as bad. I used to spend hours standing near the shirt racks wondering what, if anything, would match the slacks and ties I already owned. And I rarely made the right choices.

Then one day I had an idea. I had two friends who loved to shop. So I invited them to do my shopping for me. We turned the whole thing into a party. The three of us dashed off to the nearest shopping mall for an hour and then came home and ordered pizza. The next time we took other friends with us and turned the event into a major shopping spree. It was great fun.

I have a friend named Kayce who had to take a certain math class in college. She didn't like math, but she wanted good grades, and she was determined to do her very best in the class.

Imagine how she felt when on her first test she received a D–.

Now Kayce was a good student. She worked hard and studied hard. And receiving a D– made her mad. She decided that not only was she going to pass the class but that she was going to get an A.

Going back to the beginning of the book she began studying harder than ever. She read every page, worked out sample problems in the margins, and checked her work. Whenever she missed a problem, she went back and worked on it until she could do it right. She spent more time studying math that semester than all the rest of her classes put together.

And the work paid off. On the next test she received a B. The next time, an A. And she finally passed a test with a perfect score! (She aced the next test, too, but because she had learned the material so well she skipped a couple of steps and was docked five points, even though she had the right answers!)

By buckling down to her work, Kayce took her most difficult class and turned it into her easiest. And because she was doing so well, it also became her favorite. She had such a good experience that she eventually majored in math in college and became a junior high school math teacher.

As you continue to look for the good in yourself, remember that if you have problems that can't be ignored, sometimes they can be made to work for you. Try it! Take a positive approach to the problem. Discover the satisfaction of conquering a difficult problem and turning it into an asset.

How to Get Started!

- Take stock of the things that worry you most about yourself. If you can, forget them. But if they are things that just can't be ignored, look for ways to turn them into strengths. Find ways to make them work for you.

5

IMITATING THE BISHOP

DISCOVERING YOUR TALENTS, PART ONE

One! Two! One, two, three, four!"
Jon Cameron flashed his right hand in a vigorous downbeat as the high school jazz band began playing a snappy tune. A trio of saxophones took the lead while trumpet players hit notes above the staff. The band was playing in a region music festival and was playing a piece that Jon had arranged himself. Holding his trumpet in one hand, Jon conducted the band with the other.

After a few minutes, Jon turned around and stepped to the front of the stage. He ran his fingers over the trumpet valves and licked his lips. Then he lifted his trumpet and blazed into an exciting jazz solo. His fingers danced over the valves, and his face darkened a shade as he played higher and higher up the scale.

And then, suddenly, there it was! High C! Jon hit the note perfectly and held it, his face growing darker and darker by the second.

Finally, when it seemed that smoke would come pouring from his ears at any second, he sent the note blazing up another octave and released it.

The audience of high school musicians cheered wildly. Jon smiled and waved, then returned to his place at the front of the band.

I could have listened to Jon for hours. A high school senior, he had beautiful trumpet tone. Besides that, he could sight-read music, double-tongue perfectly, and hit higher notes than anyone I've ever heard.

Jon had an edge over most of the musicians he played with. He had started playing the trumpet in fourth grade, so he was well ahead of his class when he entered junior high. Besides that, he had taken piano lessons for several years, which gave him a solid musical background.

But there was more to it than that. Jon had a musical sense that went beyond lessons and practice. He had a talent for playing the trumpet.

I know a young woman named Sandy who's the same way in ballet. She began taking lessons when she was in eighth grade, and by the time she was in high school she was dancing with ballet students at a local university.

She eventually went to college on a four-year scholarship, and even before she graduated was dancing in productions with a professional dance company.

"I know other dancers who work just as hard as Sandy does," one of her teachers told me. "But they'll never be quite as good as she is. Sandy has natural strength and flexibility that other dancers have to work for. And she has a sense of rhythm and timing that can't be taught."

Like Jon, Sandy had a talent for what she did.

There are as many talents in this world as there are people. Some people have a knack for making things. Others have a flair for sports or music. Some have talents in art.

When I was in school I had a friend named Rhett who was a whiz at matn. He didn't study any harder than anyone else, but he always had the best scores in the class. Numbers just made sense to him. He had a talent for math.

I had another friend who could impersonate famous people. When he'd call me on the phone he'd use a John Wayne voice and say, "Well hello, pilgrim. This is the Duke calling." He could do almost any movie star you could think of, and he could do a few others things, too, like water sprinklers, fire engines, and telephones. Paul could imitate perfectly our bishop's distinct, southern drawl. Sometimes he'd call other boys in the priests quorum, tell them he was the bishop, and ask them to prepare a talk for sacrament meeting that week!

Now you've been blessed with talents too, lots of them. You might have a beautiful singing voice or a flair for acting. You might be a natural at the piano or on the tennis court. Perhaps you have a way with people or with animals.

Some of these things may be obvious. But many of your talents will lie hidden beneath the surface, waiting to be uncovered. If you want to find them, you have to look.

Finding your talents isn't always an easy thing to do. But if you approach your search with the right attitude, it can become an adventure of discovery.

Here's what you need to do.

Start by considering things you like. It's possible that the Lord blessed you with talents for things you have no interest in, but it's not likely.

So make a list of things you like to do. Include everything you can think of. Do you like music? Write it down. Do you like sports? Then write that down, too.

As you do this, don't be afraid to list general ideas as well as specific ones. The fact that you enjoy being with people may seem like a vague idea, but list it anyway! It will give you a place to start from.

The next step is to analyze each item on the list. Break it down. Make it more specific.

If you listed music, for instance, pinpoint exactly what it is about music that you like. Is it singing? Playing an instrument? Writing tunes or lyrics? Or just listening?

Even vague ideas like being with people may have a root somewhere. Try to find it! Do you like talking with others? Listening? Counseling? Telling stories? Whatever you decide may be the root of an undiscovered talent.

Once you've pinpointed your interests, dig a little further into each one. If you like singing, for instance, try your hand at singing! Join a chorus. Start a quartet. Make a tape. If you like art, sign up for lessons. Show your work to an artist. Enter an art show.

This is the most important step of all, for this is where you'll discover where your interests actually coincide with your talents.

I know a young woman named Jennifer who enjoyed swimming. She loved being in the water, and she liked learning new strokes. So when she was in seventh grade she joined a local swimming club. She won several meets against other clubs, and she went on to swim for her high school team, too.

Jennifer found that she had a talent for swimming, and after high school she even began coaching at the same club she started out with.

I know another young woman named Char who liked music. She had taken piano for several years, and she loved performing. So she began experimenting with other instruments. She learned to play the violin, and she did so well that she was able to teach many of the younger students.

And then she tried the mandolin. She found that the mandolin wasn't really much different from the violin, and she became good at it, too. She played in a bluegrass quartet at a ward talent show one time, and she played as if she'd had years of experience.

As you dig into your interests, don't worry if things take a little time. Even though Jon, the musician we met at the first of this chapter, had a talent for music, he didn't just walk into the band room and begin playing jazz ensembles. He put a lot of hard work into his music before he was able to refine the abilities the Lord had given him.

I first discovered that I had an interest in writing when I was in fifth grade. And I wrote stories all through junior and senior high school. People told me that I had a way with words, and teachers often encouraged me to pursue writing as a career. But it wasn't until I was in college that I sold my first story — twelve years after I first began writing.

If it seems you have a flair for something, don't give up if it takes a little time to polish it up.

It's also important that you don't become discouraged if some of your interests don't pan out. Many of them won't. Singing and drawing are both high on my own "Like to Do" list. But these are both examples of interests that don't match my abilities. I have a terrible voice, and I can't draw much better than a five-year-old.

I don't let that bother me, though. I have other abilities, and rather than worry about singing and drawing, I concentrate on things I *can* do.

And don't minimize any of your talents just because they seem small or insignificant. Being a good listener or being able to make people smile are just as important as being able to sink a thirty-foot hook shot or play a Mozart concerto.

When I was in college I had a friend named Ana. She had the most beautiful, carefree smile I've ever seen. And having her smile at me was all it took to make me feel like a million dollars. I don't know what other talents she might have had, but her smile blessed my life. I'm thankful that the Lord gave it to her.

Your own smile might bless other people, too. Or your laugh. Or your ability to listen. These might seem like simple things, but if the Lord gave them to you, he had an important reason for doing it.

Once you've discovered a talent, make the most of it. Use it. Polish it. Refine it and make it the best you can. Use it to bless your life. Use it to bless the lives of others.

I live near a young man named Marty who's a terrific artist. He loves drawing caricatures of people, and in his more serious moods he enjoys making intricate pencil drawings of mountains and wild animals.

Most of all, he loves sharing his talents. When someone he knows is having a bad day, Marty will whip up a cartoon to cheer him up. When one of his friends has a birthday, he'll draw her a hilarious birthday card. And at parties, he'll sit in the corner with his sketch pad and draw caricatures of all his friends and their dates.

The Lord didn't give Marty the ability to draw just so that he could decorate his own bedroom with pictures. He wanted Marty to use his talent to bless the lives of others. And that's exactly what Marty does.

And that's what you must do, too.

If you can sing, then sing! If you can act, then act! Find opportunities to use your talents. Find opportunities to polish them and make the most of them.

Every talent the Lord has given you represents an opportunity for you to excel. Each strength and ability you develop gives you a chance to rise above mediocrity. Take advantage of them.

I have a friend named Mary Kay who's a skilled dancer. In her studio is a sign that reads, "100%." When I asked her what it meant, she said, "Every time I come in here, I give my dancing 100 percent. I don't hold back. I give my dancing my very best effort."

You should do the same. Work at your talents until they begin to work for you.

Remember that your interests are only a place to begin looking for talents. And not every one of them will pan out. But as you earnestly and prayerfully begin searching for them, you'll find that many of them will lead you to talents that your Father in Heaven intended for you to develop.

You'll find that the Lord has blessed you richly. And you'll begin to see why that person in the mirror really should be your very best friend.

How to Get Started!

- Make a list of the talents that you know you have. Think hard and be honest. Resolve to do your best in making the most out of each of them.

- Now make a list of your interests. Make it a long list, and include everything you can think of. Then pinpoint the root of each one.

- Next, begin digging into the items you've listed. Give each one your best effort. See if you don't have a natural flair for some of them.

- Remember not to become discouraged if some of them don't pan out right away. Some of your strongest talents may take a lot of work to get polished just right.

- Don't forget the help of your Father in Heaven. Ask his help in your search. Rest assured that he will bless your efforts to discover your talents. That's why he gave them to you!

6 *MEETING SAM THE DO-IT-ALL*

DISCOVERING YOUR TALENTS, PART TWO

*L*arry Murdock looked like he was having a good time, but I knew that he hadn't danced with anyone all night. Leaning back against the gymnasium wall, he was tapping his foot in rhythm with the band, smiling, and once in a while sneaking a brownie from the refreshment table.

So after a while I walked over to talk with him. "How come you're not dancing?"

Larry shook his head. "Don't know who to ask."

I couldn't help laughing. The gym was so crowded that many people were dancing in the halls outside. There were dozens of girls Larry could have asked. But rather than ask any of them, he spent all night tapping his foot and eating brownies.

Unfortunately, Larry looked for his talents in pretty much the same way. He did nothing. And he never really became good at anything.

I have another friend named Sam who's just the opposite of Larry. He tries everything. When he got into junior high, he tried out for everything there was. He went out for the football team (and got cut). He tried out for track (and got cut). He joined the chorus (and was tolerated, though everyone knew that he couldn't carry a tune). He ran for seventh grade president (and lost, though he was elected vice-president of the eighth grade the next year). Finally he found himself with a part in the school play. And he was great!

The funny thing was that Sam wasn't bothered by his failures. After all, he wasn't out to be a football hero. He just wanted to find out if he could play. When he was cut from the track team, he didn't feel bad. He simply had wanted to discover if he had any talent as a runner. And he succeeded in finding out!

I've always liked Sam's approach to finding talents. He failed at many things. But the more things he tried, the more talents he uncovered.

Now, the Lord has given you talents, too. Many of them. And He wants you to find them and use them. The best way to start looking is by digging into your interests, as we discussed in the last chapter.

But many of your talents may lie in areas you might never have thought of. Finding them can be an adventure filled with fun and excitement.

My friend Sam the do-it-all is a perfect example of this. Besides all the things I mentioned earlier, he joined the chess club. He joined the science club. He took karate lessons. He didn't know anything about chess or science or karate, but he was eager to learn.

Later on, he learned to paint. He tried playing the drums. It seemed that every time he turned around he was trying something new. He wasn't successful at everything he tried, but in the process of exploring, he learned many new things about himself. He dis-

covered that he had a knack for swimming and painting and many other things, too.

And he had a whole lot of fun along the way.

When I was in college, I met a young woman
named Lynn who was the same way. Lynn was having a difficult time deciding what she would do for a
career. So she tried a little bit of everything. She took
modeling lessons and joined the predental club. She
took a course in photography. She tried her hand at
newswriting.

Lynn eventually settled on a career in advertising,
but not before sampling many, many other possible
careers. Some people might claim that Lynn wasted
a lot of time in her search, but I don't think so. And
neither does Lynn! She'll never pose for magazine
covers, but she can help her friends to look their best.
She'll never be a professional photographer, but she
can still take pictures at parties and weddings.

Take a few minutes and look around for new things
that you can try, too. Then try them just for the fun
of it. And when you find things that you like—and
that you're good at—stick with them. Get good at
them.

One day I was walking through a bookstore and
stopped to browse through the sports section. I was
surprised at how many books there were and how
many different sports they covered. There were books
on football, baseball, basketball, hockey, boxing,
racquetball, tennis, golf, wrestling, weight lifting,
hiking, camping, backpacking, climbing, track and
field, swimming, diving, karate, downhill skiing,
cross-country skiing, shooting, fishing, fly fishing,
and riding, just to name a few.

There were dozens of books on sports I'd never even tried before.

I bet there's a few sports on that list that you've never tried, either. And I bet there's a few of them that you could be good at.

So try a couple! Even if it's just for the fun of it. Who knows? You might find a talent for something you knew nothing about. And at the very least you might find yourself with a new hobby.

A couple of years ago when a bunch of my friends were planning a skiing trip, a girl named Lisa asked if she could go. She had never skied before, but she was anxious to give it a try. So we took her along.

On her first run, Lisa spent more time in the snow than she spent on her skis. (It reminded me a lot of my first run!) But by the end of the day she was skiing as well as many people do after several lessons. She had a sense of balance that made her a natural on the slopes.

Lisa skied with us all that year. And she was good. Sometimes we'd be standing on the edge of a steep hill, wondering if we were really brave enough to ski it, when Lisa would suddenly let out a whoop and go bombing past us.

It was embarrassing to have a beginner doing that to us, but Lisa was a natural on skis. She had a talent for skiing. And she had tried it on a whim.

When I was in college I one day found myself needing an extra physical education credit. I was working as a sportswriter at the time, and I wanted to try my hand at a sport I knew nothing about.

So I signed up for water polo.

Most of the other students in the class had played

water polo before, so I felt like an eighth grader playing on a high school team. Besides that, my hands weren't big enough to palm the ball, which was a major disadvantage.

But I had the time of my life! Splashing around the swimming pool for a couple of hours every day, playing in simple tournaments, and even officiating once in a while were great. I found that I didn't have any particular talent in water polo, but I did pick up an exciting hobby. It was an exciting, refreshing diversion.

Even if you don't think you'd like sports, there are hundreds — even thousands — of new things you could try. How about painting, for instance? Or music? (I would love to learn to play the guitar. I spend a lot of time in the mountains, and there's nothing I'd like better than to strum a guitar while I'm sitting around the campfire. That's one of the next things on my list!) You could try macrame, wood carving, photography, gourmet cooking (let me know if you try this one!), sewing, or singing. You could sign up for a class in a foreign language, or maybe learn about auto mechanics (if you find you have a skill with cars, I'd like to know about that, too).

The list could go on and on. Next time you're in the library or bookstore, stop in the how-to and hobby sections and see how many different subjects there are. Aren't there a couple of things that sound even a little bit interesting? If so, then try them!

And don't worry if your exploring seems to take you in a hundred different directions. When you're starting out, diversity is great. And the more things you try, the better.

When I was in high school, I knew a young man who channeled all of his energy into wrestling. And it paid off for him. He won the state and region championships in his weight, and he won many invitational meets, too.

"Wrestling just happens to be my number one thing," he once told me.

"What's your number two thing?"

He didn't even smile. "There is no number two thing."

After high school, though, he failed to earn a spot on his college team. And he suddenly found himself with little to do. He had focused so much attention on wrestling that he had never cultivated any other interests.

That's why it's okay to let your imagination run wild. Try lots of things. Not only will that give you things to do during the "off" seasons, but it will help if an injury ever prevents you from continuing a particular sport or activity.

A few years ago I discovered an interest in water sports. I learned to waterski, and I took scuba lessons. I had always liked swimming, but my interest quickly became an obsession. For a whole summer I spent every weekend boating and diving, and I often went out on weekdays after work, too. I was having so much fun with my new hobbies that when fall came I couldn't bear the thought of giving them up. I waterskied clear to the end of October, which can be quite an experience in Utah.

Finally, though, I knew it had to end. The water was just getting too cold.

It was sad, sure. But then I remembered winter sports. And after the first snowfall I was dividing my time between downhill and cross-country skiing.

My final suggestion for finding your talents is to investigate the talents of your friends. There's nothing more fun than sharing a talent or a hobby with friends. So find out what sort of things they like to do, and see if there's anything you might try, too.

When I was in high school, I loved archery. I practiced shooting several times a week, and during the winter I shot in tournaments nearly every weekend.

Now I don't know if archery is anything that you'd like to try. But the only reason I started is that my best friend was a member of an archery club.

I started rock climbing for the same reason. I had a friend who climbed and rappeled all the time. His home was filled with ropes, chocks, carabiners, and all sorts of other climbing equipment. (His family's living room featured an elegant rock fireplace. When I went to visit, I sometimes found him climbing up the side of the fireplace, clinging to the rocks like an overgrown bug!)

At any rate, I began climbing with him and loved it. And I got good at it. Eventually I even ran my own rock-climbing course.

So look around and see what talents your friends have. Find out what sort of things they do in their spare time. See if there isn't a favorite talent or hobby of theirs that you might be good at, too.

As you begin to explore the world around you, you'll discover an entirely new side of yourself. You'll uncover talents you never would have guessed you might have. You'll find yourself with a whole new list of hobbies.

Then, as you become more aware of the skills your Heavenly Father has blessed you with, your feelings of self-worth will increase. You'll realize that there are *many* things that you're good at. You'll find that you *are* an important, valuable person.

You'll come to know that you *do* have a friend in the mirror!

How to Get Started!

- Make a list of things you've never done that you'd like to try. Make it as long as you can, and let your imagination run wild.

- Now circle three things from your list that you could try this week. Then try them! And remember that this is an adventure. Do it just for the fun of it!

- Don't let fear stop you. If there's something that you'd like to try, then try it! Don't waste any time worrying about what other people might think.

- Take a look at the things your friends are doing. See if there isn't a talent of theirs that you might be good at, too.

7 *TRYING OUT FOR THE JAZZ BAND*

OVERCOMING FEARS

*F*or the tenth time in five minutes, Mindee Creer was checking her hair. She looked to be sure the ribbon around her skirt was straight and then took a deep breath to relax herself. Finally she peeked again through the window of the ice cream store.

Mr. Westphal, the manager, was still on the phone.

Feeling a twinge of disappointment, Mindee turned away but didn't leave. Mr. Westphal had to have a free minute sometime, and when he did, Mindee was going to ask him for a job.

Mindee had turned sixteen just a few days before, and she was anxious to have her first job. She wanted to be able to buy her own clothes without help from her parents, and she wanted to start saving money for college.

Her best friend, Teresa, was just as excited. "Come down to the ice cream store," she told her. "We've got an opening, and I know you'd love it there. Mr. Westphal is wonderful to work for!"

Mindee had gone to the store that very afternoon, but she arrived at a busy time. She was afraid to approach the manager with so many people looking on.

The next day was almost as bad. Several people were trying to decide between flavors, and Mr. Westphal was taking an order for an ice cream cake. It seemed that the manager was always busy with someone.

For a while, Mindee thought about giving up. "By now he's probably hired someone else," she thought. "And it wouldn't be good to bother him when he's so busy, anyway."

Fortunately, Teresa was quick to straighten her out. "A lot of people have applied for the job," she said. "But he hasn't made any decisions yet."

Besides that, Teresa had told Mr. Westphal all about Mindee, and he wanted to meet her. After all, Teresa was one of his best employees, and he was anxious to interview one of her friends — especially if she was anything like Teresa.

And so, for the third day in a row, Mindee was at the ice cream store. She waited for another minute and then peeked through the window to see that Mr. Westphal was finally off the phone.

Mustering up her courage, Mindee walked boldly into the store and right up to the manager. Her heart was pounding, and her face was flushed, but she managed her most confident smile.

"Hello, Mr. Westphal? I'm Mindee Creer. I'd like to apply for a job."

The store manager smiled warmly. "Mindee? Why, you're Teresa's friend, aren't you? Come on in! Teresa's told me all about you!"

Within minutes, Mindee and Mr. Westphal were talking like they had known each other for months.

She squealed when he offered her the job, and she ran home feeling almost dizzy with happiness.

"He was holding the job just for me!" she said. "And I was almost too afraid to ask him for it!" She squealed again. "I can't believe I kept putting it off for so long!"

Have you ever had an experience like that? Where you've been scared to do or try something, only to find out there was nothing to be scared of?

I have.

Fear is one of the greatest obstacles in discovering your best self. It keeps you from trying new things. It keeps you from meeting new people. It keeps you from discovering your very best self.

Learn to rule your fears!

I know a young man named James who played tenor saxophone in his high school band. His school had an excellent jazz band, and James desperately wanted to join.

But he was afraid to audition.

"I was just too shy," he said. "I didn't know if they really needed another sax or not, so I just kept putting it off. I kept making up excuses not to go in."

Even so, James had prepared himself well for an audition. He memorized all of the required scales and practiced so that he could play all of them in less than sixty seconds. He could play the chromatic scale perfectly, and he practiced sight-reading and tuning.

Then finally, midway through his junior year, he made an appointment with the band director and tried out. He was accepted with no trouble, and by the end of the year he was a section leader.

"Playing in the jazz band was the best thing I did

in all of high school," he said. "And I'm sorry I didn't audition earlier. I really missed out."

I know a young woman named Sherrie who had a similar experience. But hers didn't end quite so happily. Sherrie wanted to try out for the school swim team, but by the time she became brave enough to try out, it was too late.

"I'm sorry," the coach told her. "But we've already been practicing for several weeks now. You might try us a little earlier next season."

Neither James nor Sherrie had anything to worry about. But their fears kept both of them from trying out for a long time. James was lucky enough that putting off his audition didn't hurt his chances. It just kept him from enjoying himself a little sooner. Sherrie, on the other hand, was not so fortunate.

Don't let it happen to you!

If you want to discover the best that is within you, you've got to give yourself opportunities to grow and to learn. You've got to take chances once in a while and try things that seem scary.

Don't put these things off! Do them now!

One time I took a group of young people from my ward water-skiing. Everyone was taking turns out on the water and having a good time except for a boy named Glenn.

"I'm just a little nervous about being up on the skis," he told me. "I'm afraid of crashing. I don't want everyone to laugh."

"No one's going to laugh," I assured him. "And we all crash. That's half the fun!"

I didn't want to force him, but I knew he'd have a great time if he'd just get out in the water and try it. So I kept after him and finally convinced him to give it a chance. He got up right away and had so much fun that we had to drag him out of the water so someone else could take a turn.

"That was great!" he shouted from the swimming platform. "I wish I'd gone earlier!"

Most fears work out just like that. You spend hours—or even days, sometimes—worrying about something that didn't turn out to be bad at all. And if you're like me, you end up wishing you hadn't wasted so much time putting it off.

I have a friend named Jeff who is a senior in high school. He desperately wanted to ask a girl named Catherine for a date, but he was too shy. (Haven't you heard this one before?) After all, he didn't really know Catherine, and he wasn't sure if she even knew who he was. Besides that, he thought that maybe she already had a boyfriend.

"Now you're just making up excuses," I told him. "Go call her."

So he called. And it turned out that Catherine *did* know him. She was so excited to go out that she decorated his locker one day and even baked him cookies.

Jeff was amazed. "Where's she been all my life? I should have called her weeks ago!"

I'm sure you've heard stories just like that before. So have I. In fact, I've had the same thing happen to me. The only difference is that I never dated the girl I liked until several years had passed.

I really missed out that time.

Now how many things do you suppose you've missed out on, just because you were afraid?

Promise yourself that you won't let it happen again!

When I was in junior high, I had a friend named Bryant who wasn't afraid of anything. Whenever a teacher would ask a question, Bryant was always the first one to raise his hand. Even if he wasn't sure that he had the right answer. Bryant loved to participate, and he knew that giving the wrong answer once in a while never hurt anyone.

At dances, Bryant was the same way. Rather than waste his time worrying if any of the girls liked him, he'd march right out on the floor and ask the cutest girls he could find. He got turned down more than anyone else, but he danced more than anyone else, too.

One time a bunch of us were attending a college basketball game. Before the game started, we were standing near the railing watching our favorite players when someone let out a shout.

"Look! There's Bryant!"

All of us looked to see Bryant standing right in the middle of the team. He had hopped over the railing and had just enough time to get several autographs before a security guard came to shoo him away.

As I watched him, I couldn't help remembering the time I had been lucky enough to ride with one of my favorite players in an elevator. I had been too shy to even say hi. If Bryant had been there, he'd have struck up a conversation and talked him into coming to one of our own junior high games.

There have been many times since then that I've followed Bryant's example. One time, for instance, I was deep-sea fishing off the coast of Mexico. We were on a large fishing boat, and I wondered what it would be like to drive it.

So mustering up my courage, I climbed up to the wheelhouse and asked if I could drive the ship. The captain looked surprised, but after a moment he grinned and nodded. And the next minute I was steering the ship.

Another time I was boarding a DC-10 from Salt Lake City to Los Angeles. I'm a pilot myself, and I longed for a peek at the flight deck. This was at a time when most airlines were beefing up their security, and I doubted that I would be given the chance.

But then I thought about Bryant. And I knew that whether he succeeded or not, if he wanted a look at that flight deck, then he wouldn't get off the plane without asking.

So after we reached cruising altitude, I approached one of the flight attendants.

"I was just wondering if I could see the flight deck," I told her. "I'm a private pilot, and I'd really like to meet the pilots."

The attendant laughed and told me it was against the rules.

I was disappointed, but I felt good that I had been brave enough to ask. And when the plane landed, the flight attendant returned and told me that since we were on the ground the pilots were willing to show me the cockpit.

When I was in high school, I had a friend named Kathy who loved to paint. As part of a school project she drove to a local university one afternoon to visit a traveling art exhibit. The art building was open as usual, but the room with the exhibit had been closed early that day.

Kathy was disappointed, but as she looked through the window she noticed someone—possibly a custodian—walking around inside the exhibit room. She knew there was a chance he would let her in, even if it was just for a few minutes.

So, gathering up her courage, she tapped lightly on the window. The man inside walked over and opened the door.

"I'm sorry to bother you," Kathy said. "But I didn't know the exhibit was going to close so early today." She took a deep breath. "I drove a long way to see this. I wonder if you'd let me look around for a few minutes."

The man was surprised.

"You came all the way just to see the exhibit?"

Kathy nodded.

The man smiled. And he let her in. As it turned out, he wasn't a custodian. He was the artist himself. And he was so flattered with Kathy's interest that he gave her a guided tour through the exhibit.

"It was wonderful," Kathy said. "I met one of my favorite artists. I got to spend a whole hour with him looking at his paintings. And all I had to do was ask!"

If you really want to discover the best in yourself, don't let your fears rule you. Don't let them stand in the way of your dreams and goals. Don't be afraid to seek those things you want.

Resolve to start now! Ask the question! Seize the opportunity! Take the chance! Make the call!

Do it now.

How to Get Started!

- Think of something that you've been putting off because it seems a little scary. Go do it. Now!

- Overcoming a fear can be a refreshing, invigorating experience. Try this: Think of someone you often see and would like to know but whom you are afraid to speak with. Do you know someone like that? Now, the next time you see that person, go right up and say hi. Ask how his or her day has been. And see if you don't walk away feeling ten feet tall.

- Remember President Kimball's favorite saying: "Do it!" Make yourself a card to post on your mirror or on your desk where you can see it often. Except make yours say, "Do it NOW!"

8 *SKIING IN THE FOG!*

CHARTING YOUR COURSE

*L*istening to Chris Davis always made me feel good. The energetic ninth grader could chatter like a squirrel and talk for hours without ever saying the same thing twice.

At the moment he was outlining his plans for the future. "I have two plans," he said, stirring a milkshake with a plastic spoon. "Plan A and Plan B."

I leaned back in my chair and got ready to listen. "What's Plan A?"

Chris sampled a spoonful of his milkshake, nodded, and became very serious.

"Plan A starts in high school. I'm going to take all the math and science classes I can, and maybe get a few college credits out of the way. After I graduate, I'll take a year of college, go on a mission, and then get back into Brigham Young University and major in biology. My goal is to earn a doctorate at Scripps Institute. And someday I'd like to do research on whales."

He grinned. "I'd really like to study sharks up close, too. But I think that would get a little scary!"

Even so, it sounded like such a good plan that I was anxious to hear Plan B.

Chris took a moment to dig a lump of ice cream from his milkshake before telling me about it.

"Well, in Plan B, I'll still take a lot of math and science courses. But this time I'll put a lot more emphasis on music. I play the cello, you know. So after my mission I'll go to Brigham Young University on a scholarship and major in music. I'd like to play with the Boston Philharmonic, and someday I'd like to teach at a university."

Chris's plans were pretty well thought out for a ninth grader, but then that's the way he was. He liked making plans for the future and dreaming of things he might do.

I had known Chris for two years, and I had always been impressed with his ambition. He had earned money by doing odd jobs and mowing lawns since fifth grade, and he had been on the honor roll nearly every term of junior high school.

"I decided that I never wanted a career that didn't require good grades," he told me. "So I decided in seventh grade that I would always get the best grades I could."

The thing I liked about Chris was that he always seemed to know where he was going in life. And he usually had a pretty good idea of how he was going to get there. He could tell you what he was doing the next night or the next week, and he often had a pretty good idea of what he'd be doing the next month or the next year, too.

And that's a good way to be.

I remember asking a friend of mine one Monday what he had planned for the weekend. He just laughed. "You want to know what I'm doing this weekend? I don't even know what I'm doing tonight!"

It's funny how many people make this same mistake. They fail to make plans for the next day or the next week, so they usually end up doing nothing. Worse than that, they sometimes fail to make *any* plans for the future, and they often end up doing nothing at all. Ever.

Don't let that happen to you!

Several years ago I was guiding a group of teenage boys on a nighttime cross-country ski trip. There was heavy fog on the mountain that night, and as we skied across a large alpine meadow, the boys became completely disoriented. In the fog there were no landmarks to see, and no one had any idea which direction to go.

Without a guide, many of them would have become lost in the fog. Many of them would have spent the night skiing in circles, and many wouldn't have gone anywhere at all. Few of them would have reached their destination.

Life is a lot like that. Without having something to guide them, many people wander in circles all their lives, never going anywhere. They become unhappy because they lead aimless lives. They spend their lives wondering which direction to go, and they achieve only a fraction of their potential.

If you really want to find the best in yourself, you've got to know where you're going in life. You've got to take a good look at yourself and decide what things are important to you. You need to begin thinking about what directions you'd like to take.

Remember that there's no rush in setting major

goals for your whole life. But it's good to start thinking. It's good to have dreams to think about and goals to work toward.

I used to spend a lot of time in the mountains with a man named Bill. He was a first-class whittler, and in just minutes he could transform a block of aspen wood into a lifelike carving. He could carve horses, ducks, fish, people, or anything else he wanted.

I was always amazed at his skill, and I once asked him to show me how he did it.

Bill took a chunk of wood and held it out.

"The first thing you have to do," he said, "is picture in your mind what you want to whittle. Try to see the finished product. Then just carve away until you've got what you pictured."

And that's what you must do. Picture the person you want to become, and then work away until you become that person.

Now you may not have your whole life's work planned out yet. And that's okay! Our world is changing fast enough that you may be preparing yourself for a career that hasn't even been invented yet.

But in the meantime there are things you can be doing. There are many personal, short-term goals that can get you moving in a positive direction.

Start by listing four or five areas that you'd like to improve in. School might be a good place to start. Or track, or music, or art. You might want to upgrade your social standing or improve your appearance. You might want to be a great debater or a better team captain.

If you're like me, you might have dozens of areas that could stand improvement, but for the moment, just single out four or five. You can always go back and pick up some of the others later.

Now, next to each item, describe what you'd like to achieve in that area. Be specific. Write down exactly what you'd like to be, how you'd like to be thought of, and what you'd like to do.

If you listed school, for instance, you might jot down the grades you'd like to get and the courses you'd like to take. You might write something like this: "I want to be on the honor roll every term and finish the year with a 3.5 GPA. I especially want an A in English so I can be on the yearbook staff next year."

If you're shooting for a better social standing, you might list those people you'd like to be friends with and those clubs you'd like to join. And your paragraph might look something like this: "I want to be popular! I want to go to every dance this year, and I *don't* want to spend another Friday night watching television!"

As you write these things, don't be afraid of describing how you really feel. After all, no one's going to see your list but you, so there's no need to be embarrassed.

And don't be afraid to reach for the stars. You're not really setting any goals here, so there's nothing wrong with letting your imagination run wild. Just be honest and list those things that you really want.

Now comes a crucial step. Consider the things you've written. Then list those things you can do *right now* to achieve them.

Under school, you might write: "To earn my 3.5 GPA, I spend time after school every day doing homework. I finish each of my assignments as neatly as possible, and I do them all before going off with my friends. I get to know my teachers and let them know that I value their class. I don't procrastinate."

Under friends, you might write this: "I am a genuine friend. I don't gossip or backbite, and I'm always positive. I listen when my friends talk, and I take their problems seriously. I let my friends know that I care about them by doing things for them, by telling them that I like them, and by being honest."

(Notice that these are written in the present tense. Writing them this way makes them more immediate. It will help you to begin doing them *now*.)

After you've done this, read carefully what you've written. Think about each statement.

Now do them! Take time every day to review your statements. Give yourself credit for the things that you're doing well, and identify those things you need to work harder at.

As you do, you'll find new purpose and direction in your life. And you'll feel a boost of satisfaction as you come closer to your dreams.

A couple of years ago, several friends of mine set off on a mountaineering trip. They wanted to reach the top of a distant peak, and because it was a point that was easy to see, they rarely relied on their map or compass.

As they hiked, though, thick pines and jutting hills often kept the peak out of sight. Sometimes they'd emerge from the timber to see that they were off course.

By setting goals for yourself, you can avoid this danger. Even listing a few areas of improvement will give direction to your life. It will give you a course to follow.

Not only will these things give you a sense of purpose and direction, but they will boost your confidence when you reach them.

Many people dream of being someone better, but few ever do anything about it.

Be one who does. Start now! Think often about what you want from life and how you intend to go about getting it. Find those things you can improve in your life, and go about improving them.

As you do so, you'll find your life filled with direction and purpose. You'll find yourself with things to do when there's nothing to do.

Most of all, you'll truly come to find the best in yourself.

How to Get Started!

- Think of four or five areas of your life that you'd like to improve. List each one on the top of a piece of paper.

- Next to each item, describe exactly what you'd like to achieve in that area. Be specific. And be honest—don't be afraid to describe those things you really want, no matter how impossible they might seem.

- Now consider each item carefully. Then list those things you can do *right now* to achieve them. Write them in the present tense so that you get the feeling that they are things that you really are doing.

- Have you done that? Okay—now follow through! Do them!

- Review your list often. Keep your dreams and plans in mind. Monitor your progress. Keep working!

- Don't worry if you feel like changing goals from time to time. As your life changes, so will your dreams and interests.

- Look forward in life. Try picturing where you want to go and what you want to do. Let that picture give you direction and guidance.

9 *YOU'RE GOING TO DO IT WHEN?*

THE "AS IF" PRINCIPLE

Collette Morrey slammed down the telephone and whirled around to face the man across the room. Her teeth were clenched, and her face was red.

"How dare you!" she demanded. "How dare you do this to me!"

Kenneth Hadley, dressed in a suit and holding a briefcase, tried to look innocent. "But honey—"

"Don't you *honey* me!" Collette shouted, holding her arms at her sides and clenching her fists. "You promised me this dinner *weeks* ago!"

Kenneth set his briefcase down and held out his arms.

"Now, don't do this to me, sweetheart. I've *got* to go to New York. You *know* that!"

"You've *always* got to go to New York!" Collette snapped, withering Kenneth with a murderous glare. "You've always let your work come first!"

Collette and Kenneth, both actors in a community theater, continued their argument so skillfully that I was entranced as I watched them. From my seat in the first row of the theater, I could see their expressions perfectly, and I could hear every word they said. They were so good that I kept forgetting this was a play and not a real fight.

After a couple of minutes, Collette finally stormed from the stage and the lights went out. It was intermission.

During the break, I took a few minutes to stretch and look around. There were just four people in the audience that night. It wasn't because it was a bad play but because this was just a dress rehearsal. The play didn't open for another week.

But as I watched the stage crew preparing for the next scene, it was clear that no one was treating this as a rehearsal. The actors played each scene as though they were being watched by hundreds of people. The stage crew dashed on stage between scenes, changing props and hurrying to finish before the next cue. Sound and lighting technicians took care to see that everything was done just right. No one had the attitude that this was just another practice. They were treating it like the real thing.

There's a good reason for that. Because if an actor can't do it in practice, he usually can't do it for real, either.

Now there's a good lesson in that. If you can't learn to be happy now, you probably won't be able to be happy later in life, either. If you can't learn to find success in your life now, there's no reason to think that you'll be able to find success later.

Many people fool themselves into believing that later is always better. Next time is always a better time to start. Next year things will be different.

Don't let yourself fall into that trap! If you can't do it now, you won't be able to do it later, either.

Maybe you're trying to be a better student. Or maybe you want to be a better athlete. Perhaps you'd like to be a better friend. If you work long enough at it, there's every chance you'll make it.

But there's no reason to wait. Start *now*. Act now as if it's already happened. Act as if you've already become those things you're striving to become.

If you're trying to become a better dancer, for instance, do those things that better dancers do. Join a dance club. Audition for a show. Try out for a team.

If you want to be a better student, do all the things good students do. Start taking notes in class. Turn your assignments in on time. Go to your teachers when you need extra help.

Don't wait for a better opportunity.

When I was in junior high, I had a friend named Bruce. One day he was talking about his plans for the future.

"I want to get a scholarship to college," he said. "So when I get into high school, I'm going to work and study *hard.*"

Now Bruce was not an extraordinary student. He got by in most of his classes, but his grades weren't exceptional. This wasn't because he couldn't do the work but because he didn't do the work.

"When I get into high school, though, I'm really going to buckle down," he said. "Junior high doesn't matter all that much anyway."

It was good that Bruce was making plans for the future. But his mistake was putting things off until later. If he were really serious about getting a college scholarship, he would have started right then to prepare for it. He would have worked in junior high just *as if* those classes were vital in earning his scholarship.

In a very real sense, his junior high classes *were*

vital. After all, they gave him information that would have made future classes easier. They gave him opportunities to refine his learning skills and to learn good study habits.

Several years ago a friend and I began taking scuba lessons together. Our instructor emphasized safety and spent a lot of time drilling us on emergency procedures. He made us practice buddy breathing and clearing our masks and regulators. One time, twelve feet underwater, he even turned off our air tanks so we could practice making emergency ascents without air. And he had no tolerance for anyone who took the practice sessions lightly.

"Someday you *may* run out of air below the surface," he told us. "You won't think it's a laughing matter then, and I don't want you to think of it as a laughing matter now."

When I was learning to fly, my flight instructor was the same way. Even during the most routine training flights he quizzed me constantly on emergency procedures.

"Where would you land right now if you suddenly lost your engine?" he'd ask, right in the middle of another conversation. He'd study my choice of landing sites, offer suggestions, then quiz me some more. He made it clear that good pilots were always prepared for the unexpected.

One time we were droning lazily along when the engine suddenly began to sputter. A cold chill washed over me, and I quickly followed the procedures he had taught me. Because we were losing power, I lowered the nose of the plane to maintain a safe airspeed, then turned to my emergency checklist.

"Carb heat . . . on. Fuel mixture . . . rich. Fuel shutoff valve . . . OFF! It was off!

Positioned on the floor of the plane between the seats, the valve that controlled the flow of fuel from the wing tanks to the engine had been switched off. My instructor had managed to shut it off, simulating an engine failure, without my knowing it.

For a few moments, I believed that we really were losing our engine. And I treated the emergency like it was real because I thought that it was real! That was a valuable lesson for me, because since then I have made three emergency landings for real. The first time, my instructor was in the plane with me, but the other times I was all on my own. I had no one to help me.

I'm glad I didn't have to wait for the real thing to learn what to do!

If you want to be a good student, don't wait until you get into Mrs. Peterson's biology course before you start to get serious. Don't even wait until next term.

Start now! Start now and work as if every assignment you do is the one that will determine whether you get that scholarship.

If you want to be a good athlete, don't wait until you get that new helmet or that new pair of Gameblaster running shoes. Don't wait until you make the varsity team.

Start now! Jump into your training like you're contending for the all-star team. Give every practice your very best shot.

And don't stop there! Do all the other things that successful athletes do. Be the first player on the field before practice and the last one to leave when it's over.

Think of yourself as a good athlete, or as a good student, or as a good musician.

I know a young woman named Corinne who moved to a new school midway through her junior year of high school. She was anxious to have a fun, successful year. But she knew that making new friends sometimes takes a long time.

So rather than wait, she went to school each day as if she already had friends. She'd sit next to people on the bus and talk with them as if they'd known each other for years. She'd talk with people in class as if she already knew them. She'd sit with people at lunch as if they ate together every day. And it wasn't long before those people *were* her friends.

When I was in the Missionary Training Center preparing for my mission to Japan, I knew a young elder who didn't understand this principle. He was having a hard time concentrating on his studies, and he had a hard time learning his lessons.

"I just take a little time to warm up," he said. "But once I get into the mission field I'll be all right."

At the same time there was another elder in my district who was just the opposite.

"I'm on my mission *right now*," he often told us. "And I'm going to work like it."

And he did. He devoted all of his time and energy to learning lessons, learning scriptures, and learning culture. He made certain that by the time he left the MTC he was as prepared as he could be.

The trouble with many people is that they keep putting things off. They believe that things will always be easier later. They believe they'll do better later. They believe things won't matter until later.

The sad thing is that later never comes. It just stays . . . later!

I was talking with a young man named Tyler one time who wanted to improve himself physically. He had a good exercise program planned out, but because it was winter he decided to wait a few months before starting it.

"It's just too cold now," he said. "But once the weather warms up, it'll be easy."

It never happened, though. Spring came, then summer, then fall, and then winter again. And Tyler just kept finding reasons to believe that later would be better.

Except that later never came.

Don't wait for later to come! Act as if this were your last chance. Picture the type of person that you'd like to be, and act now as if you've already made it. Strive to be what you wish to be thought to be.

And as you do, you might find that you have already made it!

How to Get Started!

- Picture the type of person you'd like to be someday. And picture the sort of things you'll be doing when you make it. Well, don't wait! Start doing those things now. If you think you'd like to be a better musician, then start acting like one. Take lessons. Practice hard.

- Never use the word *later*. When an opportunity comes to you, don't wait for a better chance or a better time. Go after it *now*. Act as if this is the best chance that you'll ever get.

73

- Think of something that you've been putting off for a better time. (There's bound to be something!) Then act as if this were your last chance to do it. Get it done!

10   *HOW TO WIN WITH A BROKEN WRIST*

BELIEVING IN YOURSELF

You've got to be kidding!"

Robert Jacobs looked from the doctor to the nurse and then back to the doctor again. He could tell by their faces that they weren't kidding.

"Great," he said. "Two months before state, and I break my wrist."

The number one singles player on his high school tennis team, Robert was having his best season ever. He was ranked among the top five players in the state and was the top-seeded singles player in the region. He was practically a shoo-in for the state tournament.

And then, while helping a neighbor, Robert had fallen from a ladder and fractured his right wrist. The wrist he played with.

"It just figures, doesn't it?" he asked. "I mean, it's like Murphy's law—if you drop a piece of toast, it falls with the buttered side down, right? So if I break my wrist, of course it's the one I play with!"

Knowing that he had to wear the cast for several weeks, everyone assumed that Robert's tennis playing was over for the year. Everyone, that is, but Robert.

"It really bugged me," he said. "I'd worked hard to get as far as I had. I'd put a lot of time and effort into my game. And I wasn't ready to give it all up yet."

So Robert went out with one of his teammates and tried playing left-handed. And he realized that he just might have one more shot at the state tournament.

"I've always hit a strong, two-handed backhand," he explained. "So hitting a left-handed forehand came easy. Besides that, I've always had good speed on the court—I've got quick feet—and I've always been good at strategy. I knew that if I could just get my serve down, with a little luck and a lot of work, I still had a chance."

Robert knew that rejoining his team as a lefty meant starting at the bottom and working his way back to the top all over again. And that was hard for someone who was used to being number one. Besides that, he'd have to requalify for the varsity team before he could qualify for the region tourney. And he'd have to win at region before he'd be given a chance at state.

"I had all the odds stacked against me," he said. "But I had one thing in my favor, and that was the most important thing of all. I *knew* I could do it."

As it turned out, that was all the edge Robert needed. He believed in himself. And that belief motivated him. Working harder than ever, he re-earned a spot on the team. He qualified for the varsity team as the number two singles player. He took third place at the region championship and went on to state, where he lost in the second round.

Robert didn't win the state championship, but he hadn't set out to do that, either. He had simply vowed to qualify and play in the tournament. And after overcoming many odds, he did just that.

All because he believed in himself.

Now there will be times when you'll face some pretty tough challenges, too. School may be a trial, and maybe you'll lose a friend or two. But at times like those, you've got to believe in yourself.

No matter how bleak things may seem, no matter how gloomy life might appear, believe that you have the power to ride things through. Even when you can't think of a single thing that's right about you, believe that those things are there, somewhere.

When I was working on my pilot's license, I spent hours preparing for my written exam. I had heard horror stories about how hard it was, and I was determined to do well.

On the day of the test, I walked into the flight school and calmly arranged my materials. I made sure I had enough scratch paper. I checked to be sure my pencils were all sharpened. And then, when everything was ready, I switched on my calculator.

Pffft!

The display flashed and went blank.

"Oh, fine!" I thought. "The batteries die right when I need them most."

For a moment I was on the verge of panic. After all, I hadn't even started the test yet, and things were already going wrong!

But then something occurred to me.

"What's the big deal?" I asked myself. "I can do this without a calculator. I was a college math major, for heaven's sake!"

77

Losing my calculator was an inconvenience, sure. But it didn't ruin me because I had a secret weapon.

Me!

Now whenever things seem to be going wrong in your life, remember that you have a secret weapon, too. You!

So learn to count on yourself. Believe in yourself. No matter how hard things may seem, believe that you have the power to slug your way back to the top.

I have a friend named Ron who was told he'd have to have his four wisdom teeth removed before going on his mission. All four teeth were impacted, which meant that each would have to be removed surgically.

The dentist told him that it was a painful procedure, and he scheduled the surgery for a Monday so that Ron could have a whole week to recover. He told Ron to take the entire week off, because he wouldn't feel able to go to work or school. Ron didn't understand any of this.

"How can it hurt that bad?" he asked me. "I broke my leg in two places once, and it didn't hurt *that* bad."

Ron had had other experiences with pain, too. He'd been bitten on the leg by a German shepherd once, and it had taken several shots and many stitches to fix him up. Another time, a panful of hot grease had spilled over his arms, burning him badly.

Now *those* things had hurt! And Ron couldn't understand how having a few teeth removed — even surgically — could be so devastating.

And he was right. He didn't need any of the pain-killers the dentist prescribed, and he was back to work and school the next day.

Later he asked the dentist about it.

"You were so convinced it wouldn't hurt that your mind probably just blocked out the pain," the dentist told him. "You were so convinced it couldn't hurt that it didn't."

Now how would *you* like to do that? Well, you can. Your mind is a powerful thing. And when it's convinced it can do something, there's almost no stopping it.

I know a young woman named Pam who was on the brink of finishing college. She was preparing for her final semester when she discovered that she needed more credits than she was able to squeeze into her schedule. Besides that, the university had a rule limiting the number of classes she could take in a semester.

Pam was told that her only choice was to postpone her graduation until she had completed the two classes the next semester.

Now Pam already had a good, well-paying job lined up. She would lose it if she didn't graduate on schedule. Besides that, she couldn't see paying nearly a thousand dollars for the next semester's tuition, just so she could take two classes.

Well, Pam did a little research and discovered that she did have another option. She could take the remaining courses through a special home-study program.

Now most home-study courses are just as rigorous as the regular college classes. Pam was required to study just as hard. She was required to write just as many papers. She was required to take just as many tests.

The only difference, in fact, was that she also had to teach herself. There was no one to help her with difficult concepts. There was no one to go to with questions.

"When I weighed the pros and cons, though," she said, "I knew I had to try it. I had to graduate on schedule. I had to take the classes."

Besides just finishing the classes, Pam was striving for a high grade point average. So in addition to completing the classes, she needed to do well in them.

"I knew from the beginning that I was in for some hard work," she told me. "But it was important to me, and I had to do it. I knew that if I just buckled down for that one semester, I could do it. And I knew it would be worth it. I knew it would pay off."

Pam convinced herself that she would be able to complete the classes. Whenever she felt overburdened, she'd take a moment to relax and then tell herself: "I can do this! I *know* I can do this!"

And she did. She finished each of her classes on time and was able to graduate on schedule.

Her greatest ally was her attitude.

I have a friend named Todd who plays shortstop on his high school baseball team. An all-around player, he can steal bases, hit like a bear, and run down infield balls like a racehorse. He takes away more would-be base hits than anyone I've ever seen.

During a game against a visiting school, a batter snapped a chopper straight toward left field. Charging after it, Todd swooped down on the ball like an eagle hoping for test-pilot status, and while still moving toward third base, he turned and rifled the ball to first.

The ball beat the runner by a whisker.

There were other good players on the team, but many of them lacked Todd's confidence. They sometimes seemed afraid to charge the ball, almost as if they'd rather miss it completely than come close and make a mistake.

But not Todd. He always wanted to be in on every play. He always wanted the ball hit somewhere in his direction. And when it was, he'd blast right after it. He gave every play his best shot.

After one game I sat and talked with him in the dugout. "You play with more confidence than anyone else on the field," I said. "How come?"

"I just believe in myself," he said. "I know I can play. And that's the attitude I take with me into the game. I go out there knowing that I can do it."

That's the attitude you need to take, too. Go into your own games knowing that you belong there. Begin every day knowing that there's a place for you, for your talents, and for your abilities.

Confidence is a virtue that will help you to go far in life. When you believe in yourself, others will feel it. They'll come to believe in you, too.

More important, when you believe in yourself, your own attitudes will change. You'll find it easier to feel proud of yourself. You'll find it easier to be happy with yourself. You'll find it easier to go after those things you want from life.

Finally, you'll find yourself doing more things and finding more successes than you ever would have thought possible.

All you have to do is believe!

How to Get Started!

- The next time you doubt your ability to do something, try this. Close your eyes and say to yourself: "I can do this! I know I can do this!" Keep saying it until you believe it.

- Start every day knowing that you belong there. Believe that there's a place for you. Know that there's a need for your talents and abilities.

- Don't let the doubts of others stand in your way. Remember that if *you* believe in something, then that's all that really matters.

11 *AND NOW – THE AVALANCHE EFFECT!*

MAKING THE COME-FROM-BEHIND WIN

*C*arolyn Lee watched the judges' table carefully. Her opponent, a fiery gymnast named Stacy, had just completed the most stunning beam routine that Carolyn had ever seen.

"She was doing things I'd never even seen before," Carolyn said. "She started out with two back handsprings, and her side aerial was just incredible! She didn't even wobble!"

Carolyn shook her head. "She was so good that girls on *my* team were even cheering!"

And then the judges announced their score: 9.6.

Without needing to add up the points, Carolyn knew that Stacy was leading the competition. She knew that Stacy would certainly win the beam, and her score would put her out in front in the race for the all-around, too. She would be hard to beat.

With two events to go — and behind by eight-tenths of a point, Carolyn knew that she had a lot of catching up to do. But she also knew that she had the bars and the floor exercise coming up. They were her best events. She knew she would score well in them.

Approaching the bars, she lifted her hand, smiled

for the crowd, then began the routine she had spent many months perfecting. Kipping up to the high bar, she whipped her heels and cast into an elegant handstand. She swung forward, folding her legs to miss the low bar, then straightened again as she flew up into another handstand.

Pulling herself into a pike now, she swooped downward, missed the low bar, then kicked into a front flip with a half twist.

She landed perfectly.

"It felt so good!" Carolyn beamed. "It went just the way I wanted it to! It gave me the points I needed to catch up."

Carolyn's score beat Stacy on the bars, moving her two-tenths of a point closer to first place.

And all she had left was the floor exercise.

"I knew I was still behind," she said. "And I knew I'd have to do the floor perfectly to win. I didn't have any room for error. I knew I couldn't make any mistakes."

And she didn't. She completed her routine perfectly, putting so much power and personality into her performance that she had the audience on its feet cheering when she was finished.

Being behind by so much, many athletes would have felt tremendous pressure. After all, coming from behind to win isn't all that easy. And under pressure, many athletes wouldn't have been able to perform at their best.

But Carolyn was different. Rather than slow down, she put every last bit of power she had into her performance. She went into her routine knowing that she could still win.

She refused to quit.

I know a young woman named Susan who had a similar experience in tennis. During an important meet, she found herself trailing two games to one, and she was losing in the fourth set.

"It didn't bother me though," she said. "I mean, I'd been behind before and still won. There was no reason to think that I couldn't do it again."

So, settling into her game — not wasting any energy worrying about the score — Susan plugged away at her opponent, slowly earning enough points to win the set, the game, and finally, the match.

Making a come-from-behind win is one of the most exciting things in sports. There's just nothing like watching a team redoubling its efforts to overcome and win.

When I was in junior high, my basketball team played a team from a rival school. They jumped out to an early lead, and by the end of the quarter were ahead twenty-one to fifteen. Our coach told us to settle down, but it didn't work. By halftime we were behind thirty-seven to twenty-three.

Then during halftime, something interesting happened. Our coach took a minute to look each of us in the eye, then asked, "Why are you losing this game?"

When no one answered, he asked, "Aren't you quicker than they are?"

We nodded.

"And don't you shoot better than they do?"

We mumbled, "Yes."

Coach Brimhall's voice went up a notch. "And don't you run the best offense in the league?"

"Yes!"

The coach was speaking louder now. "And don't you run the best defense?"

"YES!"

"And Don't You Deserve To Win This Game?"

"*YES!*"

"AND ARE YOU GOING TO WIN THIS GAME?"

"YES! YES!"

"WHO'S NUMBER ONE?"

"WE ARE! WE'RE NUMBER ONE! WE'RE NUMBER ONE!"

Within minutes our coach had us so fired up that we could have beaten the Boston Celtics if we'd wanted to. We tore onto the court in the third quarter and played so fiercely that even we were surprised. We rattled our opponents, and that pumped us up even more.

We took the lead two minutes into the final quarter and didn't look back. We won the game forty-five to forty-one.

That was one of the most exciting games of my life.

But making come-from-behind wins in the game of life can be just as exciting.

When I was in high school, I had a friend named Troy who one day found himself behind in the game of life.

"It was weird," he said. "Everything that could go wrong, did. And all at the same time, too!"

It started when Marsha, one of the school cheerleaders, called to cancel a date to the junior prom so she could go with someone else. Then Troy lost his place as section leader in the school band to a player who was a grade younger than he was—a blow to anyone's ego!

And to top things off, his history teacher sent a failing notice to his parents.

"A senior in high school, and I'm still getting grounded!" he moaned. "I almost can't believe it. But then again, I'm to the point where I know that anything bad that *can* happen, *will* happen."

I knew how Troy was feeling. After all, there have been many times when I've felt the same way. Haven't you? There are times when it seems that everything is going wrong all at the same time and that the only solution is to give up. And that's why I admire Troy for the way he handled things.

"I just started calling girls until I found another date," he said. "I wanted to go to the junior prom, and I wasn't going to let one girl's rudeness ruin it for me. And Marsha? I'm glad she called! Dumping me for someone else was pretty mean, and I really don't want to date girls like that."

He didn't take his demotion in the band quite so lightly. Troy had worked hard to become section leader, and he was determined to win his spot back. So practicing every night, he worked until he had the rough spots smoothed out of his music and then challenged the new section leader to a rematch—and won!

And the failing notice? That part really took a lot of work. After taking his parents to school and meeting with his teacher, Troy made up the assignments he had missed. He retook a test or two and by changing his study habits brought his standing up to a more acceptable level.

The point is that Troy didn't give up when everything seemed to be going against him. Despite all the evidence to the contrary, Troy knew he was still full of good. He still liked himself. He knew he could still pull things off.

And so must you.

Like Troy, there are going to be times in your life when you'll feel behind, too. You might lose a friend or find yourself in some sort of difficulty. Projects you work hard on might suddenly fall apart. But at times like these, don't give up!

Most people simply quit when things aren't going their way. They let down when things aren't going right or when they're losing badly. They work the least when they need to work the most.

But remember that the only way out of a slump is to work harder! Attack your problems with all the energy you can muster. Make the come-from-behind win!

I have a friend named Tim who has an interesting theory when it comes to problems.

"Whenever things go wrong, they all go wrong at the same time," he explained. "I call it the snowball effect, but in real life it's usually more like an avalanche."

I knew what he meant! I was having a bad day once, and it seemed that everything that could go wrong, did go wrong.

It started before I even got out of bed. I slept through my alarm, so I was late for school (and got in trouble). I misunderstood a chemistry assignment and turned in the wrong page of work (and got lectured). I was having trouble in another class and asked a friend for help when I shouldn't have been talking (and got yelled at).

And this was all before lunch!

By the time school was over, I didn't want to go to baseball practice (I probably would have broken my leg). And I didn't want to go to work (I probably would have been fired).

The real trouble with days like this is that they make you feel bad. They make you think less of yourself. Sometimes they can even convince you not to like yourself.

But that's when it's most important to fight back!

Whenever things are going wrong for you, don't think less of yourself for it. After all, everyone has problems. Everyone makes mistakes.

So fight back. Make the come-from-behind win!

I remember once reading about a basketball game played between the seniors and sophomores at St. Peter's High School. As you might imagine, the game turned out to be a pretty heated contest. The seniors, in fact, played so aggressively that by the time the score was tied at thirty-two, all but one of them had fouled out.

Now, how would you like to be in *that* player's position? How would you like to play against a team of feisty sophomores? Especially when you were outnumbered five to one?

I'm sure many players would have given up. But not this one. Refusing to quit, he charged back into the game and not only kept everyone on the other team from scoring, but he made three more points himself to win the game thirty-five to thirty-two.

Don't give up when things seem to be going

against you. Don't stop trying, even when there seems to be no hope. Remember that being behind is nothing new to most of us. We all have times when everything decides to go wrong all at once.

But that's not important! It's *how we act* and *what we do* when we're behind that matters.

Don't give up when life gets hard. Instead, fight back! Put your faith and energy into the battle.

Make the come-from-behind win!

How to Get Started!

- Think of a time when you've made a come-from-behind win. Remember how it felt? Believe that you can do the same thing again.

- The next time you feel behind in the game of life, don't give up. Fight back! Muster up every last bit of power you have and give it one more shot! Make the come-from-behind win!

12 HOW TO TALK WITH A HURDLER

LETTING OTHERS BRING OUT THE BEST IN YOU

Susan Hayes hit the slope at a sharp angle and sent a cloud of snow bursting into the air. She carved her skis hard into the snow and zig-zagged through the mogul field like a ski racer going for the gold.

"All right!" she cried. "This is great!"

Blazing through the last of the bumps, Susan folded into a tuck and shot down the chute. She waited until the very last instant before digging her skis into the snow and skidding to a stop. Her face was flushed with excitement.

"Wow!" she shouted. "That was fantastic!"

The snow wasn't really all that good that day, but Susan was having the time of her life. She attacked every hillside with the energy of a whirlwind, roaring over the slopes like a person fleeing Bigfoot.

It didn't matter to her that the slopes were icy and hard to ski that day. And she didn't mind that the sun was hidden by the clouds. She was excited to be outdoors. She was happy to be alive. And she made me feel the same way.

Once, I was standing at the top of a small hill when she skied up beside me.

"You know what I like to do?" she asked.

"What?"

"This!"

And with that, she pushed me into a bank of powder and went barreling down the slope. By the time I had picked myself up, she was nowhere in sight. I skied slowly down the mountain, knowing she might be hiding in the trees somewhere. And I was just beginning to think that she'd given me the slip when SPLAT! A snowball hit me just behind the ear, and Susan was once again zooming down the hill.

Even though skiing conditions weren't the best that day, Susan was having a good time. And being with her, I was having a good time, too. She brought out the best in me.

Susan had that same effect on me off the slopes, too. One time I called her on the phone.

"Hi, there!" she boomed, even before she knew who she was talking to.

"Hi, there," I replied. "How come you're so happy today?"

"I'm *always* happy," she shot back. "And I'm especially happy now 'cause I'm talking with you!"

From the moment I began talking with her, I was as happy as she was. How could I not be? Her energy and enthusiasm were contagious, even over the phone.

I first met Susan when we were in a play together. She was a talented, experienced actress, and I was doing my first play. I was nervous about acting with someone who was so good, but she put me at ease right away. More than that, she built my confidence.

"You're so good!" she told me after one rehearsal. "I can't believe this is your first play!"

I could! Throughout the rehearsal I had stumbled over lines, forgotten my cues, and tripped over props.

"But everybody does that!" Susan assured me. "Believe me, you're terrific!"

Susan had a powerful influence on me. She had an electric personality that charged me full of life. She filled me with confidence. She made me feel good about myself.

When I was serving my mission in Japan, I had a companion who was just like that. Elder Larsen had the dynamic, energetic personality of a bottle rocket, and he had a positive attitude that just didn't quit.

One morning I woke up to the patter of raindrops against the window.

"Oh, great," I thought. "Rain."

Rain always made missionary work hard because we had to ride our bikes everywhere we went. And even though we had umbrellas and rainsuits, we always ended up getting soaked to the skin.

Besides that, not many people like to invite rain-soaked strangers into their homes. So meeting new people was always difficult.

I was gearing myself up for a long, hard day when Elder Larsen suddenly came bounding out of the shower.

"Look, Elder," he said. "It's raining! Everybody's going to stay home today! We're going to find hundreds of new investigators!"

I knew Elder Larsen was just trying to make the best of a bad situation. But it worked. When he began humming the missionary song from *Saturday's Warrior,* I finally broke down and grinned too.

Besides being a hard worker, he was full of life and fun. Sometimes, when we were approaching a door he would say, "Okay, Elder, quick: describe the person you think is going to answer the door!"

I'd think fast. "Let's see. It's going to be an older woman wearing a full-length kimono and geta."

He'd shake his head and say, "No, I think it'll be a teenage boy wearing his school uniform."

And then we'd wait anxiously to see whose prediction came closest. Elder Larsen is the only elder I ever knew who could make knocking on doors such fun.

The people you associate with have a great effect on the way you feel about yourself. People with a zest for life can turn your frown into an ear-to-ear smile. People whose lives sparkle with energy and enthusiasm can soon have you out of the dumps, too. They can bring out your very best self.

Seek them out!

I once spent a miserable afternoon on a tiny island with a boy named James. We had been boating when we got caught in the middle of a storm. Knowing it was too dangerous to try making it back to shore, we beached the boat on a nearby island and took shelter beneath a clump of willows.

As I turned my back against the storm, James caught my eye and grinned.

"Well," he said. "At least things aren't going to get any worse than they are now."

No sooner had he said that than the wind picked

up. Rain lashed the island. Our boat rocked on the waves just a few yards away.

After a few minutes, James turned to view the storm. "Well," he said. "At least it can't get any worse than this!"

Almost instantly a crack of thunder boomed over the island. The rain pounded us with renewed intensity. Gusts of wind lashed our faces.

James had to shout to make himself heard.

"Don't worry! There's no way it can get any worse than this!"

Hailstones the size of marbles suddenly began crashing all around.

James just shook his head.

"Well—"

"James!" I shouted, cutting him off. "*Please* don't say another word!"

As he looked at me, a torrent of rain cascaded off his hat. We both laughed.

The hours we spent huddled on that island could have been the worst of my life. But James, with his glued-on smile and uncanny knack for bad prophecies made it an adventure. When the storm finally broke, we motored our way back to camp in good spirits, anxious to tell our friends about our adventure.

The world is full of people who look for the bright side of things. Anywhere you go will be people who can laugh at themselves and share with you their good feelings and humor.

Find them!

It doesn't matter if they're older than you. And it doesn't matter if they're younger. Dynamic personalities are infectious enough that spending time with anyone like that is certain to bring your best self forward.

How can you *not* feel good around people like that?

When I was going to college, I worked part-time as a sportswriter. Once I was interviewing a hurdler named Jennifer in my office. It was the first time I had ever talked with her, and right away I sensed the dynamic personality that made her such a great athlete.

For one thing, she was a nonstop flurry of action. And for another, she talked like there would never be enough time to say everything she wanted to. You see, most . . . people . . . talk . . . like . . . this.

ButJennifertalkedlikethis.

She talked so fast that my pencil almost smoked as I tried to write down everything she said.

"Ilovethehurdles," she said, bouncing out of her chair and springing across the room to inspect a picture on the wall. "Imean,they'resoquick,so explosive!"

She padded back behind my desk and scored a basket in the trash can with a wad of paper. "Mymom worriesaboutmyhurdling, though. Shetoldmethatif Ievermissedonethatwouldbethefinish, thelastdance, thefinalcurtain."

I stopped writing and looked up, not knowing what she'd just said.

"What?"

Jennifer laughed and slowed down. "She told me that if I ever missed a hurdle she'd make me quit."

I had been with Jennifer for only a few minutes before I was feeling as full of life and energy as she was. And when I drove home that night I felt like I was sitting on top of the world. I was determined to write the best story I had ever written. Not just an exciting, well-written article, but a rock-'em, sock-'em, razzle-dazzle, turn-up-the-music-and-dance-in-the-hall story that Jennifer would be proud of.

Being around Jennifer not only made me feel good but it made me want to go out and be just as enthusiastic and energetic as she was. It was inspiring.

But just as people with Grand Canyon smiles and firecracker personalities can brighten your life, people with negative attitudes and gloomy dispositions can often do just the opposite. It's important that you don't forsake such people: they may need your help.

But if you're truly looking for the best in yourself, if you really want to be you at your best, it's vital that you associate with people who bring your best self out.

Soon after I graduated from high school, I discovered that I didn't seem to be going anywhere in life. I had a job and was planning on a mission, but there wasn't much more to it than that. And I noticed that most of the friends I spent time with were pretty much the same.

So I began spending more time with those friends who were ambitious. And my life suddenly made a dramatic turnaround. Rather than spending nights watching television, we were attending dances, ball games, and missionary prep classes.

Sometimes, when we found ourselves with nothing to do, we'd grab a deck of Uno cards and head for the women's dorms at Brigham Young University. Going up to the first door, we'd ring the bell and say: "Hi! We're playing a game of travelling Uno! We need everyone in your apartment to come out and play a quick hand with us so we can finish the whole building before nine o'clock!"

We were hardly ever turned away, and we made more friends than we really knew what to do with. And we certainly had a lot more fun than if we'd spent the night watching television.

Those friends had a great effect on me. They brought out the best in me. They fired me up and made me want to be at my best. They gave me the motivation to succeed at many things I otherwise might never have tried.

The people you associate with have a vital effect on the way you feel about yourself. Seek out people who have a love for life and for other people. Look for friends who have positive attitudes, who can look beyond their hangups and laugh at themselves.

Being around such people not only makes you feel good about yourself but also can be inspiring. It can be motivating.

It can bring out your very best self!

How to Get Started!

- Make a list of people you know who have a love for life and for other people, people with positive attitudes who can look beyond their hangups and laugh at themselves. Get to know them!

- Whenever you can, join large groups of people. The more people you're with, the better the chance that you'll make a few friends.

- Don't be standoffish. If someone you don't know strikes up a conversation, talk back! Remember that every time you make friends with someone, you'll probably make friends with all of *that person's* friends, too!

13 *RIVER RUNNING AND SNOWBALL FIGHTS*

LETTING ACTIVITIES BRING OUT THE BEST IN YOU

You gotta love it! You just gotta love it!"
Corey Gibson abruptly picked up speed and the next instant was shooting through the rapids. Waves lashed and churned the water all around him.

Even though I was just a few feet behind Corey, I quickly lost sight of him in the foam. And for the next few minutes I knew what it was like to be completely out of control. Great walls of water crashed all around, pitching me up from the swells one moment, then swinging me back into the current the next. Only my life jacket kept me from being slammed clear to the bottom of the Colorado River.

This was our second day in Cataract Canyon, and this was our third trip through this same stretch of rapids. Ron Cutler, the tour leader I worked for, was letting our passengers body-float the rapids. Finding a mild stretch of white water, he beached the boats, made certain everyone's life jackets were snug and secure, then sent them down the river on their own.

Everyone loved it. And I did, too! Booming through a boiling stretch of whitecaps, I shot up over a high wave and fell crazily before being swept downriver again.

After another moment, I was past the last surge and into smooth water again. Two or three young boys were swimming out of the river ahead of me.

"All right!" one of them shouted. "That was great!"

"No kidding!" another one yelled. "Can we do it again?"

Ron nodded. "You bet! Go for it!"

The next instant, everyone was picking his way back up the rocky shore to run the rapids again.

I always loved watching my passengers when they ran rapids. Whether they were in a boat or not, it was always the same. At first, nearly everyone showed traces of nervousness. But the instant they crashed through the first wall of water, their fears turned to delight. And by the time it was over, you couldn't have found a frown if you'd wanted to.

One time, as we were crashing our boat through a heavy section of white water deep in the Grand Canyon, one of my passengers was thrown so violently from position that he smashed his eye onto another man's shoulder.

It must have hurt terribly—and it gave him the most incredible black eye I've ever seen. But the second we were through the rapids he was on his feet, holding his arms high over his head in a gesture of victory.

"Hoooooo, boy!" he shouted. "I *love* this river!"

That's the magic of river running. It doesn't matter how many problems you have. It doesn't matter how bad you feel about yourself. After a few seconds in the foam you forget everything that's bothering you.

It makes you feel good!

Just as certain people can bring out your best self, certain places and activities can do the same thing. If you're caught up doing something fun and festive, for instance, it's hard not to *feel* fun and festive. It's hard not to be happy!

And when you're happy, it's hard not to feel good about yourself!

I once took a group of young men and women cross-country skiing. They were patients from a local hospital, and most of them were battling severe depression. All of them suffered from low self-esteem.

After a few hours, however, everyone was smiling and having fun. They laughed and joked and rolled each other in the snow.

Then during lunch, one of the boys took a handful of snow and dumped it down his counselor's neck. The counselor grabbed a handful of snow and threw it back. And the next instant the air was so full of snowballs that it looked like a blizzard. It was the most fantastic snowball fight I've ever been part of! And by the time it was over, everyone was laughing and feeling good.

Of course, you can't go bombing down the Colorado River or start up a snowball fight every time you need to perk yourself up. But what about having a good water fight? Or going ice skating? Or playing a game of racquetball?

When I'm feeling a little tired of it all, there's nothing that can pick me up quicker than a fast game of basketball. I'm not the best ball player in the world (I make more turnovers than a bakery). But a few minutes on the court is all it takes to pump me full of energy. No matter what I felt like before, after playing a good, quick game I feel as frisky as a Labrador puppy.

When you're feeling less than right about yourself, don't spend your time moping around or watching television. Instead, find activities that bring out the life in you. Do things that get your heart pounding and your blood pumping.

Do things that make you smile!

I remember coming home from a long day at school. My apartment was jammed with people when I got there. My roommate's stereo was blaring, and everyone was singing, dancing, and eating popcorn.

I immediately put down my books and joined in the fun. There was such a happy, energetic atmosphere there that night that I couldn't help feeling happy and energetic, too.

Take a minute and think about things that make you feel good, things that fire your imagination and make you feel good about yourself.

Do them!

I remember a time when my job wasn't going very well for me. I was feeling bad about my lack of progress, and no matter how hard I tried, I just couldn't seem to make things work out.

Besides that (the "avalanche effect" was really in effect this time), I had just lost a good friend. Her name was Jamie, and her friendship had meant a lot to me.

So one Saturday morning I grabbed my fly rod and fishing vest and headed for the mountains. There's a certain canyon stream I know about, and fishing is one of the most relaxing things there is to do.

I was pretty well calmed down by the time I got

into the hills, but once I started hiking and had fished a pool or two, I was feeling good. The nice thing was that as I fished I was able to think things over. I was able to make some decisions. And by the time I left, I was ready to buckle down and give it all another try.

Maybe you know a place like that, too, a place where your mind is free to think and where inner turmoils don't seem quite so pressing anymore.

When I was in college, I spent a lot of time walking across campus between classes. As I did, I usually let my mind wander, and I often came up with solutions to problems I was facing or ideas for stories I was writing.

Besides that, having that time alone with my thoughts refreshed me. It gave me a chance to clear my mind and relax a little bit.

Even now, when I'm faced with a dilemma that needs a lot of thought, I'll often drive up to campus and spend an hour or so just walking around.

Once I was asked to speak at a banquet, and I was having a terrible time preparing my talk. Every time I sat down to think about it, my mind would go blank and leave me with nothing.

So finally, with the banquet only a day or so away and with no speech ready, I drove up to the university. It was a cool, dark evening, and a light rain was falling. I began walking around as usual, letting my mind wander. I thought about many things — none of which had anything to do with my speech — and I was having a good time.

And then, without any warning, BOOM! A whole flood of ideas for my talk came rushing into my head.

And the more I thought about them, the more ideas I came up with. It was great! I went home with a whole notebook full of ideas.

When you find yourself down and needing a boost, don't spend your time doing things that will keep you in the rut. Instead, do things that will bring you back to life! Start a water fight. Go to a dance. Wrestle with your brothers.

Do things that make you happy! Try things that make you feel good about yourself.

As you do, you'll find it hard to be lonely. You'll find it hard to be sad. Instead, you'll find yourself having fun and loving the life you lead! You'll develop a greater love for yourself and for your friends.

Most of all, you'll feel terrific!

How to Get Started!

- Think of an activity that makes you happy. Something that puts a smile on your face and gets your heart beating. And the next time you feel a little down, rather than mope around, go out and have fun. Get that smile back on your face! As you do, you'll find it hard to stay down.

- Next time you have a bad day, pick up your skateboard and go for a ride around the block. Or just go for a walk. Try jogging. Or go for a bike ride. See if it doesn't help!

- Just as certain activities can get you feeling good, so can certain places. Think of places that let you feel good. How about the temple, for instance? Or a quiet spot in the mountains? Think hard until you've come up with at least one good place. And the next time your mind seems a little overwhelmed, try going there. See if the atmosphere doesn't give you the chance to sort things out.

14 *HOW TO CURE A COUCH POTATO*

BRINGING OUT THE BEST IN OTHERS

*T*here were just nine seconds left on the clock, and the Tigers had the ball on the Huskies' eight-yard line. Behind by a field goal, the Tigers needed to cap this drive with a touchdown to win the game and send them into the state playoffs.

Eric Hayes set up in the backfield while quarterback Jim Martin crouched behind center and began his count.

"Ready . . . set! Hut one! Hut two! Hut! Hut!"

The center snapped the ball cleanly into Jim's hands as opposing linemen collided along the line of scrimmage. Jim dropped back like he was going to pass and then shoved the ball hard into Eric's chest.

Eric took the handoff and charged up the middle. He spun to his left to slip a tackle, crossed the line of scrimmage, and ran for the end zone. Only two defenders stood between him and a touchdown.

Four yards to glory.

The first tackle hit Eric at the waist, lifting him with his shoulders and flipping him end over end. Eric tried to tighten his grip on the ball, but at the last second it squirted out of his hands like a greased watermelon.

In an instant, players were scrambling for the loose ball. Helmets collided and shoulder pads cracked together. There was such a pileup it was impossible to see who had recovered the ball.

Feeling suddenly sick to his stomach, Eric watched as the officials untangled the mass of bodies. A few of the Tiger players were pointing toward the end zone, as if they knew the ball was theirs.

But then the referee blew his whistle and pointed the opposite direction.

Huskies' ball!

Eric couldn't do anything but watch as the Huskies ran out the final few seconds of the ball game. His side hurt, and he felt sick. Just four feet from the end zone—four feet from a certain touchdown and the chance to win the game—he had dropped the ball!

He had never felt so terrible in his life.

After the game, Eric walked home, taking unlit side streets to avoid being seen. He had seen things like this happen to other players—with the team behind by a single point, a kicker had once missed a fifteen-yard field goal and lost the game. But he had never thought it would happen to him.

As he walked along, a car suddenly passed him and then stopped. Someone called out. "Hey, Eric! Is that you?"

Eric looked up. "Yeah."

"Eric! Where have you been? We've been looking all over for you! Come on! Get in! We've got to get you to the dance!"

Eric's friends hadn't needed to go looking for him that night. But they knew how awful he must have felt. And they wanted to show him that they were still behind him. They took him to the dance that night and, later, out for a pizza. They showed him what real friends were. They were there when he needed them.

They let him know they cared.

Have you ever had anyone do something that made you feel good? Something that boosted your self-esteem and made you proud to be you? Remember how that felt?

You can make someone else feel that same way!

I know a young woman named Shannon who played the clarinet in her high school orchestra. A skilled musician, she had beautiful tone and clear, precise fingerings.

During a state-wide musical festival, Shannon's orchestra played a piece in which she had a difficult solo.

Now Shannon worked for weeks to perfect that solo. She played it over and over again until she had it mastered. She played it so often that she soon had it memorized, and in rehearsals she played it beautifully.

By the day of the festival, Shannon had all the confidence in the world. She had her part down so well she could have played it in her sleep. But something happened she could not have planned for. Something so utterly devastating that it completely ruined the entire piece for her.

On her first note . . . she squeaked!

"I couldn't believe it!" one of her friends told me. "I had played with her ever since junior high, and I had *never* heard her squeak!"

Shannon herself was so overcome that after finishing her solo, she broke down and cried. It didn't matter that she had played her solo perfectly. It didn't matter that her orchestra won one of the top prizes.

She had squeaked!

It's hard for anyone to live with such a public and embarrassing mistake, but this mistake was worse because the director of a local university's symphonic orchestra was the festival's special guest. Not only was Mr. Horrocks a renowned conductor but he also played the clarinet himself.

After Shannon's orchestra completed its performance, Mr. Horrocks took Shannon aside to speak with her.

"You play beautifully," he said. "I hope you won't go home feeling discouraged." He looked around as if making sure he wouldn't be heard, then confided, "To tell you the truth, I even squeaked once myself!"

There's not much that could have made Shannon feel any better that day. But Mr. Horrocks did the one thing that could.

Do the same for people you know!

I was watching a high school baseball game once. Midway through the third inning, a batter bunted down the third base line, then took off like a rabbit for first.

The third baseman, pitcher, and catcher all dashed after the ball but stopped when they realized the batter would make it safely to base. After all, the ball was heading for foul territory. All it had to do was touch the line and the batter would be called back. Everything would be okay.

But at the last instant, the ball hit an unseen bump and changed course. Just an inch shy of the foul line, it stopped. Knowing that the runner would be safe on first unless something drastic happened, the pitcher dropped to his knees and actually tried *blowing* the ball over the line.

Life is often like that for many of us. We spend a lot of time teetering on the brink of success and failure. Sometimes it doesn't take more than a simple nudge to shoot us to victory or send us spinning off into disaster.

Be someone who nudges others in the right direction.

I gave a talk to a group of Scouts and their leaders several years ago. It was a short talk—just ten minutes long—but it was an important thing to me.

Afterwards, I was talking with several adult leaders when a young Cub Scout pushed his way through the crowd to shake my hand.

"I liked your talk," he said. "It was really good."

I knew it must have taken a lot of courage for that young Scout to do that, and I was touched. More than that, I felt a surge of confidence and an increased sense of responsibility. I wanted to go home and get to work. I wanted to do things that would make me worthy of such young men.

I was amazed at how much two simple sentences affected me. But I realized that I could have that same effect on others.

Every day of your life you'll see people who are struggling to find themselves. You'll see people who are picked on or abused. You'll see people who are desperate for friends.

Be good to them. Go out of your way to say hi. Go out of your way to offer a compliment.

Often, all you have to do is say something simple, like, "I like your dress" or "You really look nice today."

Even if that's all you say, you'll have told that person volumes. Most importantly, you'll have told him that you noticed. And for many people, that's often all they need.

I have a friend who really lets his problems get to him. When he has a hard day at school, for instance, he doesn't forget about his worries when he goes home but lets them gnaw at him all night long.

Sometimes we'll go to dances or parties together, and I'll know that he's had a bad day. I'll know because he'll spend the whole evening staring off into space as if no one else were around.

We were at a movie one time, and I knew something was troubling him. I hoped that maybe the movie would take his mind off his troubles, but it didn't. On the way home I mentioned that my favorite part was the scene when the runaway tank ran through the shopping mall.

Mark looked up in surprise. "Tank? There was a tank in the movie?"

One week was especially bad for him. Nothing he did seemed to be going right, and at home he was practically a vegetable. He spent hours sitting in front of the television, not really watching anything but staring off into space.

But right when things seemed to be at their worst, one of his teachers called him at home.

"Mark!" she said. "I just finished reading your essay, and I couldn't wait to talk with you! It's the most wonderful essay I've ever read!"

I couldn't believe Mark's reaction. One minute he was a couch potato, and the next he was bouncing around the room like he'd just sat on a hot grill.

The change in Mark was incredible. But it happens to people all the time.

Be willing to boost the ego of others. If you like someone's clothes, tell them. If someone gives a great talk or makes an exciting play, tell them.

Just as important, help those people who seem to be teetering on the brink. It could go either way for many of them, so don't be afraid to give them a shove in the right direction.

When I was going to school, I had a friend named Heather. Sometimes when she'd pass my desk, she'd stop and write a quick note on my paper. Usually it was something simple like, "Wow, you're so good-looking today!"

A little while later I'd open my locker to find a note taped inside the door. "I looked up the word *awesome* in the dictionary," it might say. "And there was a picture of you!"

Heather was just a regular friend, like many others I had. But her notes of friendship did a lot in making school fun for me. She did a lot to bring out my best self. Because if she thought I was awesome, then I was determined to be awesome!

Do that same thing for someone else!

Remember times when people have done things to make you feel good. Remember things that others have done to boost your ego and to improve your own self-esteem. Remember how great it felt?

Then do the same for someone else! You can bless

other people's lives. You can be a tremendous influence.

Finding the good in yourself is a satisfying process. But helping others to realize *their* potential is just as exciting.

While you're discovering the best in yourself, don't pass up chances to help others find the best that is within them, too. This, as much as anything else you might do, will help you to find a friend in the mirror.

How to Get Started!

- Think of people you know who are having a tough time. Take time to make their day brighter! Do something to let them know you care! Do something to boost their own self-esteem and make them feel good about themselves.

- Remember a time when people have gone out of their way to make you feel good. Now go do that for someone else! Do it today.

- Don't be afraid to help nudge people along once in a while. If you see someone who could be teetering on the brink, give that person a nudge in the right direction!

- Don't give up on people who may be having a hard time. Being under pressure often makes people act differently. They may not be as friendly as usual, and they may seem a little cranky. Be patient with them. Even more, let them know you care!